NEW
THINKING
ALLOWED
DIALOGUES

NEW THINKING ALLOWED DIALOGUES

Is There Life After Death?

JEFFREY MISHLOVE

www.whitecrowbooks.com

New Thinking Allowed Dialogues

This compilation, Copyright © 2023 by New Thinking Allowed Foundation.
All rights reserved.
Published by White Crow Books, an imprint of White Crow Productions Ltd.

The right of Jeffrey Mishlove to be identified as the author of this work has been
asserted by him in accordance with the Copyright, Design and Patents act 1988.

A CIP catalogue record for this book is available from the British Library.

For information, contact White Crow Books by
e-mail: info@whitecrowbooks.com.

Cover design by Jana Rogge
Interior design by Velin@Perseus-Design.com

Paperback: ISBN: 978-1-78677-228-2
eBook: ISBN: 978-1-78677-229-9

Non Fiction / BODY, MIND & SPIRIT / Parapsychology /

ESP, Clairvoyance, Precognition, Telepathy.

www.whitecrowbooks.com

Praise for *New Thinking Allowed Dialogues*

~

"This remarkable collection of interviews is jam-packed with jaw-dropping, mind-blowing stories and intimate conversations that will turn anyone's sense of reality upside down and sideways.

It's a must-read for those wishing to shatter illusions of what is possible, in this life and beyond."

~ **Debra Lynne Katz, PhD.**

"Throughout the existing literature of the 19th-21st centuries, people outstanding in a great diversity of professions, including highly degreed and respected scientists, have loaned their names and reputations to books and research about the subject of survival after death. It's clear they all discovered in some way that skeptics need their skepticism. A lot of time and energy has been fruitlessly spent in trying to convince individuals who were not interested in admitting that the fact of survival is more important than the fear-based fiction of their ego-minds. Yet this surely will change as increasingly more professionals come to their own personal spiritual discoveries, and as the world continues to grow progressively more comfortable with the realization that we all survive death. I am optimistic that the width and breadth of experience and research presented by the highly respected individuals within this current work will also continue to support such realizations."

~ **August Goforth,** author of
The Risen: Dialogues of Love, Grief, & Survival Beyond Death.

"A central purpose of religion is to teach the soul how to shape itself so it will be attracted to a positive after-death environment. But if life after death isn't real to us, it will be hard to take that task seriously. This book approaches the afterlife from two perspectives, mediumship, and the near-death experience, both of which give evidence that human consciousness survives bodily death. In so doing it hints at the unbroken Eternal Life that underlies our daily life as restricted by time—not only after, but also before and during, our sojourn in this world."

~ **Charles Upton,** author, *The Alien Disclosure Deception: The Metaphysics of Social Engineering.*

Contents

A Note from Jeff

You are reading the first in what we hope and expect to be a series of books based on interviews from the *New Thinking Allowed* channel on YouTube. In an important sense, this book is the culmination of a process that began in 1972 when I was guided by a powerful dream to pursue my interests in the paranormal by involving myself with the non-commercial segment of broadcast media. Within three weeks of that dream, I found myself sitting across a table—in the studios of KPFA-FM, Pacifica radio in Berkeley, California—conducting interviews with world class experts in human potential and consciousness exploration. These were the subjects I cared most about; and the resource of these conversations gave me the confidence to create an individual, interdisciplinary doctoral major in "parapsychology" at the University of California.

For the past half century, this interview process—largely a volunteer effort—has been the backbone and the joy of my professional life. It has allowed me to benefit from in-depth conversations with researchers and thought-leaders on such topics as remote viewing, mediumship, out-of-body experience, UFOlogy, meditation, hypnosis, mind-over-matter, the mind-body problem, and the larger implications of these topics for psychology, philosophy, health, science, and spirituality.

1

Near the end of 2020, Las Vegas entrepreneur Robert Bigelow announced the formation of a new Institute dedicated to the study of human postmortem survival. The first project of this endeavor would be to launch an essay competition focusing on the best evidence for the survival of human consciousness after permanent bodily death. Imagine my surprise when I learned that, when asked by George Knapp during a radio interview who should enter this contest, Bigelow responded by saying, "People like Jeffrey Mishlove who have spent their whole professional lives studying this question." That was enough impetus for me to devote most of the year 2021 to preparing the essay that eventually won the $500,000 grand prize.

Undoubtedly, my essay was strengthened by my access to the many video interviews I had conducted on the topic of postmortem survival. In fact, two of the interviews in this anthology (those with Vernon Neppe and Leslie Kean) were referenced in the prize-winning essay itself. But, I think it is fair to say that this particular collection, *Do We Survive Death?* offers a broader view of the afterlife and its implications, than my essay with its more narrow focus on the best evidence.

I would be remiss if I did not point out that this book is only possible due to the many contributions of volunteers, particularly those of the eight interviewees and, of course, James Tunney, whose Foreword is both comprehensive and gracious. Greta Peavy deserves a special "thank you." Greta personally was involved in transcribing all of the interviews, and she also supervises the efforts of our other volunteer transcribers. In addition, much labor was done by a volunteer committee of editors who worked with me directly to convert the spoken language of an interview into the written words appropriate for the pages of this book. The members of that committee include Laura Neubert, Emmy Vadnais, Ali Khandabagadi, and Elizabeth Lord.

Finally, I wish to acknowledge the publisher and owner of White Crow books, Jon Beecher. Jon has also been a guest on *New Thinking Allowed.* His company specializes in books concerning the afterlife. I know that for him, this work (like my own) is founded on a strong passion and commitment. So when, after the Bigelow prize was announced, he offered to be my publisher, I did not hesitate to move forward with him, knowing that we are both walking a similar path in life.

The *New Thinking Allowed* video collection[1] contains well over 1,000 interviews, with several more being added each week. These videos have collected more than fifteen million views. I hope this new imprint with White Crow books will bring in new readers to explore their incredible back catalog of titles relating to spiritualism and survival. I expect it will also bring in new viewers to our YouTube channel. Most importantly, I hope and expect that this partnership will catalyze a deeper understanding in both readers and viewers of the vast depths of the human psyche.

---

[1]   www.youtube.com/c/newthinkingallowed

Foreword

The Mystic Whisper

Yes, our lives may sometimes seem like a little vapor that appears for a moment and vanishes away. But lest we be too hasty racing to the afterlife, we must allow our vision to rise and vigorously seek a full life before our inevitable demise.

This book is not just about survival of consciousness but also underscores an enriching excavation of surprising evidence, especially relevant to our lives now. It is part of an ongoing reclamation of the territory of human encounters from a deluge of data. It can be seen as engaged in the re-balancing within science against a deadly, unduly materialist disposition.

So let me digress for a moment. It was a fine, bright blue, late-spring day in Sweden. I had been late in leaving my daughter at playschool. Fruit trees on green-gold orchard grass between the old jail and graveyard detained us. Fine margins keep us out of those places. You cannot waste such a grand morning chance for climbing when winter had been so long. I still see her clinging happily among the pink and white blossoms across from me. I like being up a tree, too, the same as the next kid.

After leaving life in academia and a legal career, in order to paint and eventually write, I was glad not to be plying my dusty books diligently. That day I was sauntering home, like drifting on the heavenly breeze, lines came formed and coherent as a golden sequence. It was as if they had floated from the crisp air and involved no cognitive exertion but reception. Maybe it was just a mind-chime on the wind in a fair clime. I am aware of the standard causal explanations for such casual occurrences, but there is a curious feature that distinguishes them over time. Such incidents may be characterized by a force which alters the percipient.

It was not overly rare for me, but the content of those sentences led me to write and commit myself to embark on an unexpected exploration of mysticism in a more determined endeavor. I simply had no expectation that I would re-align my awareness externally so profoundly and dig deep again in a sustained, individual study. For me those seeds grew, blossomed and bore fruit. It led me to re-examine many books and travel across the Atlantic. It would lead me to the wide vista of New Mexico to enter the magic cavern chiaroscuro of the host of New Thinking Allowed (NTA), informed by the ghosts of the Thinking Allowed series. Unusual, gifted insights guided Jeff in his life also.

Hosts and Ghosts

Perhaps I had originally written largely from inspiration, intuition, the right brain, or rather heard the *logos*, whisperings of the muses, spirit-guide susurrations through fruit tree leaves, my angels murmuring or even the 'man of light' associated with Suhrawardi (1154-1191). I had to scrutinize many subsequent lines and examine the content with a cold eye, the left side of the brain perhaps or a more lawyerly sense.

Was I saying anything worthwhile and, if so, how did that match the authoritative discourse on such matters? Were not such topics almost taboo in some sophisticated places? What was the benchmark in such an ancient but fluid, necessarily cosmopolitan, dynamic discussion as informed by contemporary scientific thinking? I had read much on such matters quite a while ago. Thus, a necessary triangulation led me to study the work of Dr. Jeffrey Mishlove.

He is a celebrated 'host.' That word is meaningful in the sense of covering an entertainer, a person extending hospitality, a carrier of another force including information and even a sacramental element. For me, personally, and consistent with Evelyn Underhill (1875-1941), spiritual consciousness is a good descriptor of the relevant domain he works in. Most prefer plain consciousness.

Jeff was also inspired by Underhill and directly by many more people, such as one of his mentors Arthur M. Young (1905-1995). Jeff clearly contributed to this field with *The Roots of Consciousness* (1975), which was part of the pendulum-swing away from behaviorism that had held sway for 60 years or so. I see his specialty of parapsychology at the center of concentric rings of his career in consciousness exploration. Surrounding this focus is general science, psychology, philosophy, magic, other esoteric subjects such as alchemy, spirituality and mysticism, all interpenetrating in a unified field.

Nobody in the world has created such a body of audio-visual work on consciousness, nor matched his range of serious interviews. My Swedish mother-in-law is still a little skeptical that the young man who interviewed Terence McKenna (1946-2000), Marvin Minsky (1927-2016) or Francis Crick (1916-2004), is the same chap that I call a friend now and with whom I have engaged in many interviews on NTA.

My mystical endeavors led also to a critique of scientism and technology and a discussion of the role of science and nature of intelligence. Lo and behold, Jeff had been there as well with Theodore Roszak (1933-2011), who was one of his friends who coined the term 'counterculture,' John McCarthy (1927-2011), Hubert Dreyfus (1929-2017) and Rupert Sheldrake, to name but a few. He is not a player, as William Shakespeare (1564-1616) conceived an actor, but rather a serious active scientific player, psychenaut (to use the language of another influence—Jean Houston) or argonaut in what I call the 'animasphere.'

He is a living authority, thankfully without parentheses. His work puts him on the bank by the stream of consciousness where another influence, William James (1842-1910), seems to stand in silent company at an estuary on the sea of unconsciousness in the twilight of unknown teeming shades and other seeming forms of crepuscular consciousness. If not a spirit perhaps a hologram, a subject that Jeff discussed with Michael Talbot (1953-1992).

Jeff's technique operates to give space to his interviewees while gently probing in a profound way into the littoral zone of ambiguity and inconsistency, with charm. On the firm shore of his academic knowledge, he has sharp focus. He seeks treasure in the sand of experience and expertise among the tidal pools of consciousness and the driftwood, flotsam and jetsam from collapsed waves on the strand of lives and events.

His successful essay, in the Bigelow Institute competition, marshalled the evidence for survival of consciousness in a persuasive way. I do not need to be persuaded personally, but many do. Thus, there is a great value in sharing insight, as it may help us to contextualize our own inevitably imperfect instincts. It may thaw the blinding, icy blocks with which scientism hides our perceptions. It may reclaim an awareness that materialism has sought to deride. It may legitimize a conversation that your tongue would not have been moved to make. It may lead you to investigate the dynamic discussion of topics that science has undermined.

These interviews, in written form, complement the recordings and allow more time to pay attention to a fascinating story of voyages in consciousness. One may imagine they possess that eerie sense invoked from contemplating Arnold Böcklin's (1827–1901) painting the *Isle of the Dead* (1880) or stories of sailing across the Styx. We may recall Death playing chess on the seashore in the Swedish film *The Seventh Seal* (1957) or a sense of a great ship passing in the night.

8

But these NTA stories are much more vital and life-affirming, like the scintillating stream that Jeff observes. The study and phenomenon of the spirit world is not one-way traffic but a reflexive relationship, an eternal loop, or a circle of light as one mystic poet put it.

The Golden Echo

Openness to the survival of consciousness influences one's life and approach to the nature of knowledge. In Sweden, I visited haunts of two writers very aware of the otherworld, August Strindberg (1849-1912) who wrote influential works like the *The Ghost Sonata* (1907) and Emanuel Swedenborg (1688-1772).

Perhaps their spirit insinuated in a way I never suspected. Swedenborg wrote more about the afterlife than nearly anyone. He was one of the greatest minds of all time. He is ignored in secular Sweden, despite his eminence as a scientist. In Gothenburg, the city where I live, in 1759 he famously saw a fire in Stockholm a long way away. This story is contested now of course.

It was partly out of his work in London, that William Blake (1757-1827) emerged and the spiritual movement happened, foreshadowing a widening split with Newtonian, utilitarian and imperial science. This prefigured the spiritualist revival, which many suppose came from the USA. This presumption is despite a vigorous spiritual tradition in Britain which never died and included the Second Sight skill studied by scientists like Robert Boyle (1627-1691). William James and American Transcendentalism were influenced by Swedenborg's sense of the spiritual universe, survival of consciousness and interdimensional interpenetration, and this informed their lives and methods.

Denizard Hippolyte Léon Rivail (1804-1869) is the founder of Spiritism, under the pen name Allan Kardec. He is seen as the source of Spiritism in many countries, not least Brazil. However, his Spiritism emerged from attendance at a Swedenborgian circle. Swedenborg is a profound influence and some have noted the parallel life of the great mystic Baal Shem Tov (1698-1760). In many senses, it was Swedenborg who announced the New Age, literally. Swedenborg was a neighbor to the mystic-magician Baal Shem of London (1708-1782) when they lived in the East End. This was also an age of 'orientalism' with influences from China, Persia and India.

Charles Darwin (1809-1892) and Alfred Russel Wallace (1823-1913) had their revolutionary papers on evolution jointly presented at the Linnean Society in London in 1858. This was founded in 1788 in honor of another Swede, Carl Linnaeus (1707-1778), who emerged in the same scientific circles as Swedenborg and had some family relations. Linnaeus might have symbolized the left brain as did Swedenborg the engineer, but the latter has a spiritual awakening in a tavern in London which shifted him.

Around Bloomsbury and the British Museum, a battle for the position of the spirit in science emerged. Both Blake and Swedenborg knew the area and lived nearby. Darwin lived in Gower Street just behind the Museum. He would get most credit for the theory. Francis Galton's (1822-1911) Eugenics Office would be located there. Modern psychology partly emerged here as did 'psychic forces,' which was a term proposed perhaps so it would be tolerated in the retreat from spirit.

There was clearly a shift that began in the 1860s in the 'modern' UK around this locus. Scientists like Thomas H. Huxley (1825-1895) and the X Club sought to dispirit discussion of science. They did not want to consider evidence of spiritual activities regardless of sound experiments. Scientism, involving undue extension or claims for scientific method, chilled spiritual exploration in a triumphant march to displace spirit.

Psychical research faced 'a place where a royal flush can never beat a pair,' as Tom Waits put it about unfair card games. The allegations of legerdemain at certain séances around Bloomsbury (which undoubtedly may happen as much as bad scientific experiments), were used to tarnish all. People were prosecuted and, according to Sir Arthur Conan Doyle (1859-1930), later persecuted.

We should remember that some of these open-minded scientists had decided not only to reject the notion of spirit, but to turn away from any evidence presented of its reality and persistence to pursue a policy of discrediting existing phenomena universally. These were the early days of telegraph and telecommunications and materialists believed in the imperial power of actual remote contact instead of spiritual senses. A scientific Jedi mind-trick was played whereby the perennial assumption of existence and survival of spiritual consciousness was wiped out.

Henceforth, spiritual consciousness and psychic forces would have to be proved to the satisfaction of a class who did not want it to impede their own growing prestige (which once meant conjuring). This was a clever shift in the burden of proof by the new priesthood who would not approach with open-mindedness something deemed not useful to an industrial empire. This *a priori* assumption arguably contributed to the growth of anomie and alienation in the wasteland of over-concentration on machines, materials and industrial process.

Huxley's agnosticism was not mere neutrality but a requirement that what was believed could be scientifically proven.

The dismissal of spirit comes from this period of the rise of scientific racism and the imperial criminalization of homosexuality. Writers at the time sought to counteract the new combined harvester that reaped not just religious dogma but the very concept of the spirit and phenomena of spiritual or psychic experiences. The Society of Psychical Research later sought to fill the gap in science that denial of spirit caused. The anti-spirit trend was why Alfred Wallace was obscured. This area of London was also where the saga of the conundrum of 'altruism' was played out in the life of George Price (1922-1975). In a strange twist of fate, this area was where Jeff made the acquaintance of his fellow American Ted Owens 'The PK Man' (1920-1987) at a conference in the University, precisely because of the lack of attention given to him, surprise, surprise.

Evidence of Nature and Nature of Evidence

When my mother died in Ireland, a bird flew into my room in Spain. When her mother died in rural Ireland, a bird flew into my room in the city. Are we to ignore the natural, recurrent and consistent phenomena of such things recorded from the beginning of time and would that be scientific? Those facts would be easy to prove and probabilities assessed, but the interpretation and meaning is another level of fact or reality where common causation is inadequate.

Paradoxically, those who ignore the natural are often quite willing to dismiss something as supernatural. It still comes down to facts and credibility. Law, science, knowledge and life revolve around evidence. When scientism closed its eyes to spirituality, investigation dwindled. This is one of the reasons why evidence of the paranormal or supernatural itself was ignored outside the circle of brave scientists who did look and did know.

One of the best ways to have no evidence is not to look for it. If it emerges and you are in power, you may ignore it. If persistent and you do not want it, you can smear the presenters. Still, research persisted and formed an accessible body of studies.

Law has its own consistent, coherent and reliable recording of cases. Law reports have dealt with many cases of post-mortem communication (often in the context of wills) and these may be neglected in the literature. Catherine Ann Crowe (1803-1876) wrote *The Night-Side of Nature; Or Ghosts and Ghost Seers* (1848). This included reference to a remarkable case discussing the ghost of Thomas Harris in 1791, for example. Against scientism, undue materialism and behaviorism, some have kept the embers alive.

The cumulative effect of these NTA interviews here is to help us remember and challenge a constricted worldview which denies our potential and restricts the mode of our consciousness. We can listen, evaluate and think. Now we can look closer at the text with a record that makes available to wider discourse a valuable new, written source that can create a positive feedback loop. Coming from teaching law, where evidence is critical, these NTA interviews show how valuable a gentle, respectful cross-examination or inquisition is.

Jeff interviews experts and experiencers and experts who are experiencers. There is an art to eliciting and interpreting evidence and its nature. If you are a Christian for example, you are bound to accept that the divine intention must have been to initially privilege oral communication of the events as optimum, as they were not written down for a few decades. This oral relaying was an important part of formal witnessing and recalling at the time.

If you are a lawyer you understand the significance of an interview. If you are a phenomenologist, you understand the value of this method. If you are none of the above, you still have a set of beautiful interchanges, which will inform, challenge and inspire you, personally and professionally, in relation to the mystery of existence. Courts have always respected evidence of a person involved or an expert in the area. In the early days of the common law a jury had local knowledge that was relevant to interpretation of the events. Personal witness, whether as an expert or experiencer, is of critical probative value.

Investigators in the shadowlands between this world and the next, or other dimensions, need focus and courage. They are aware that the Empire of Scientism will ridicule what (until a few generations ago) was regarded as normal from time immemorial. It is also easy to forget that heart is needed to talk of something unusual which is also personal, such as loss of one's child and husband, as in the case of Dr. Betty Kovacs. There is a sense here that clever and highly educated people bare their souls beyond personal need and pain in order to share and care for others in doing so. On the airwaves or in print, such stories may speak to some unknown person whether alone somewhere or highly aware of our remarkable potential. She applies her expertise in myth and comparative literature allied to her experience to advance understanding.

All interviewees have been successful, independently of their explorations, events or episodes presented here. All stories are impressed with the personality, life experience and witness of the interviewee. There is a spectrum of modes of involvement with afterlife communications.

One type involves application of investigation, inquiry or research of direct engagement with the afterlife. Dr. Vernon Neppe, a neuropsychiatrist, recounts a fascinating tale of a Chess Match between dimensions. It is a compelling study with interesting issues of interpretation of the evidence. Michael Cremo reminds us of Alfred Russel Wallace who saw this materialist-spiritual split. It also links to William James. Dr. Stafford Betty, as a professor of religious studies, discusses the literature on spiritualism and what lessons we might take in conduct of our lives. Dr. Alexander Moreira-Almeida, a psychiatrist, brings us to the Southern Hemisphere and Spiritism with a mixture of European and African influences. His study raises an important issue. We may misinterpret what are spiritual phenomena and pathologize activities because of a limited, scientific paradigm. Spiritualism in its physical form is also examined by Leslie Kean through the methods of direct investigation used by good journalists which uses subjective involvement.

I vividly remember a finger poking my back in a shop near the British Museum once, only to find nobody there when I turned. This place had been frequented by the magician Aleister Crowley (1875-1947) and Gerald Gardner (1884-1964) the Wiccan. Crowley had his first major mystical experience in Stockholm. Maybe there's something in the air? Unusual ceremonies took place in the basement of this shop in the past. These things are nearly impossible to prove but many have tried. Physical manifestations from the afterlife are challenging and remarkable, and invite ingenuity of experiment as shown in the work of Charles Richet (1850-1935), whom Leslie Kean refers to. This is an area where evidence makes you really wonder, question and reflect.

The continuous efforts such as those which W.B. Yeats (1865-1939) experienced or people explore still today, involving voices and even ectoplasm, are arresting and may alter the consciousness of participants. Deliberate participation or investigation in a phenomenon is complemented by potentially tragic involuntary crashes through the doors of perception. Then the witness may bring back remarkable evidence. Alan Ross Hugenot uses his engineering and physics knowledge in the interpretation of his Near-Death Experience (NDE). His interest led him to become a medium and he built on his experiential foundation as a result. The persistence of consciousness can also be explained by people who act as conduits between this world and the next.

In Dr. Eben Alexander's celebrated NDE example, he had a profound personal experience, which he was uniquely professionally qualified to assess through a paradoxical reversal of roles. Experience and expertise combine to give very persuasive, double-strength, direct evidence. A neglected field is that of animals and the afterlife. Although Swedenborg did discuss this, we might think about Yudhisthira in the ancient Mahabharata, who declines to go to paradise if his faithful dog cannot come. You may find yourself asking, "well if this is true, would I behave differently from animals?" Miranda Alcott explores the continuation of relationship after an animal dies from her extensive work in this context.

On the Foreshore

Though I have seen all these interviews and sometimes more than once, I found that the written text draws your attention to significant details that a pleasant enjoyment of a convivial conversation might miss. I found shards of evidence to be gathered again or lone leaves on the stream.

This book reflects the inquiring mind of Dr. Jeffrey Mishlove, as a source on consciousness knowledge, in synergy with esteemed explorers producing a gestalt greater than the sum of its parts.

We will witness a continuing battle with the Empire of Scientism. This is an ongoing clash resulting from a reductive, computational theory of mind, denying free will, spirit, self, personhood, and even, perversely, consciousness itself. Such a view tends towards colonization of consciousness and calculated resort to exploitative, technical prosthesis as opposed to an open-minded, properly scientific and humanistic inquiry whose object is facilitative enhancement of our mind and spirit. In contrast, this collection is some of the fruit of a lifetime of work, like olives from a tree thousands of years old pressed to yield golden oil for practical purposes. What struck me was the abiding courage that kept these interviewees and interviewer engaged in a shared quest to comprehend our humanity and personhood. An interview means to see the other or another and implies a space in between.

Similarly, this liminal, opening space of interdimensionality or threshold of consciousnesses on the foreshore between worlds is the place of becoming. We should pluck the ripened fruit and harvest the seeds sown from our curiosity about an inevitable fate that waits for us all. We too shall be winnowed on the wind. We should face our future with the equanimity emanating from persistent perennial awareness of our eternal nature as consciousness which is fundamental and from which all other enterprises spring.

Some leading 'conscious agent' theorists say that consciousness is fundamental—but not human consciousness. Our existence is in the unified light-dark, mutating multi-colored, ying-yang like Jeff's NTA symbols indicate. Consciousness is both carried in corporeal form and is of incorporeal (or perhaps what we might term excorporeal) content in an interpenetrating infinity sign. Be content. Be content by being not mere container or vehicle.

Do not confuse the vessel for the vision, veil for value, verisimilitude for verity, viaduct for viator, veneer for veridical, the noun for the verb. By releasing naïve assumptions we have a better chance to comprehend ourselves and fashion or frame methodologies to vindicate what all mystics know.

Otherwise, we will be reduced to mere conscious agents in a Procrustean, computational pattern of information and rendered redundant in a digital 'Menschenpark.' Have confidence in the gift of consciousness, look at evidence and have hope, now and forever. Whatever your starting point in your own exploration of your own consciousness and considerations of what comes next, I hope you enjoy this first written collection of NTA interviews on this important and interesting topic.

James Tunney,
November 2022,
Gottenburg,
Sweden

1

The Chess Game Beyond the Grave
with
Vernon Neppe

J**effrey Mishlove:** today's program will explore a chess game literally, beyond the grave. Dr. Vernon Neppe, a renowned international neuropsychiatrist and head of the Pacific Neuropsychiatric Institute, joins me in-studio to discuss this special event. Vernon is the author of numerous books: *Cry the Beloved Mind, Reality Begins with Consciousness,* and a trilogy of books about *déjà vu.*

Vernon Neppe: Thank you so much, Jeff.

JM: I should say something about your credentials as a chess player at the master level. You are a chess champion from South Africa and the organizer of the first interracial chess tournament there. In fact, it may be considered the first multi-ethnic athletic event in your country, if a chess tournament is an athletic event.

VN: Yes, the chess match was organized by the University of Witwatersrand Chess Club (UWCC). I was captain of the club at the time. We were approached by a group of players from Soweto. They did not have a name for their club at the time. Ultimately, they became the Soweto Chess Club and my club hosted the first multiracial sports game with this new group. While organizing the event, UWCC discovered—it was on the 15th June 1972—the tournament was legal in South Africa, provided we did not serve alcohol.

JM: I understand that, as an expert chess player, you are one of the rare individuals who has played 60-80 opponents at one time.

VN: That is true. I had some challenges in terms of playing chess exhibitions and it's rather exciting because people think, "Oh well, you've just got to look at each board." But, of course, there's planning to be considered. Strategy in chess is the key component.

JM: Beyond playing multiple opponents while looking at the chessboards, you could even play blindfolded, I understand.

VN: Yes. I used to play blindfold chess, but I must admit, I would choose my opponents very carefully. The quality of my chess-play would diminish markedly.

JM: In any case, you are a scholar with an understanding of what play at the Master or Grandmaster level is about.

VN: Yes. And I try to relate this knowledge in the context of history because our subject of discussion today pertains to events in the early part of the 20th century. Géza Maróczy (1870-1951) was the number two player in the world round about 1905. This fact is highly pertinent in relation to his 'ostensible' (let us say) match with Géza Maróczy to play Viktor Korchnoi (1931-2016). Korchnoi was, strangely enough, the number two chess player in the world in 1980, and later, became the World Senior Chess Champion.

JM: We are talking about a game that took place between 1987 and 1993, initiated by a Swiss scholar and researcher, Wolfgang

Eisenbeiss, with the idea that evidence for survival after death could be further substantiated by the agreement of a deceased spirit, one who would be willing to manifest through a spiritual medium and play chess with a living Grandmaster.

VN: Dr. Wolfgang Eisenbeiss, with a doctorate in economics in Switzerland, came up with the idea that maybe, just maybe, a chess game with Maróczy's 'spirit' would be one way to prove survival after bodily death.

JM: To my knowledge, Eisenbeiss was an amateur chess player.

VN: Yes, Jeff. I have been through Eisenbeiss's games, one or two of them, and his level of chess play is that of a good, probably grade B player. He is not bad. The reason why I went through one of his games is possibly the start of this story. It's not published but it is very interesting. I often hear, "Well, you know, this is obviously fraud by the medium Rollans." Or, I have had Eisenbeiss being accused of deceit. Ultimately, when one looks at the data, it would require a major conspiracy, if this was the case. There was even a Hungarian librarian involved. Eisenbeiss did not speak Hungarian and Maróczy's family were rather ambivalent about all of this and were involved, too. But in any event, Eisenbeiss, when he started and first interacted with Robert Rollans, the medium—

JM: —who would do the automatic writing—

VN: —initially. What happened was Eisenbeiss came up with something rather interesting. He discovered that Rollans could not play any chess and it was necessary to instruct him on the notation of chess. He could then record this during automatic writing. The reason of course is, this allows him probably to have been able to interact and do the chess stuff and know something about it, but he certainly wasn't at any kind of level where he could have produced any of the play with Maróczy.

Eisenbeiss challenged Robert Rollans, the medium to 'prove' that the game would be from the 'grave'. Fortunately, Rollans's deceased father ('Rollans Senior') was an avid chess player. Eisenbeiss, over a period of an afternoon, played Rollans Senior a chess game. Eisenbeiss recorded the game (and I have the transcript). It was overall of a limited chess standard: We (a Master, Grandmaster and I) were all are of agreement that this was very much an amateur game. But in terms of standards, you could see Rollans Senior was an average player.

VN: As for the game that began a month or two thereafter, 'Maróczy' vs Korchnoi, in terms of evidence for survival, this game has to do with a real skill at the Master or Grandmaster chess play level. That is not a skill that can be replicated by an amateur player.

Even if an amateur had studied chess extensively, it would likely be very difficult—likely impossible—to replicate the level of playing. This case has been called the number one case in terms of proof of survival after bodily death. There are several different sources that one could argue support this contention by the way they have described it. But the reason is it's not only the skills that are involved, *it is a combination of skills and data.* There was an enormous amount of data generated in the match.

JM: Let's talk about the data. I understand Maróczy, through automatic writing, was asked many questions and detailed queries about his life. For example, when he was alive as a chess player, he answered rather obscure questions about various matches and things concerning his personal life. He was able to answer these questions through automatic writing with an incredible degree of accuracy.

VN: Exactly that. They divided up these questions into general questions. like those one could find from information in libraries or from the records of chess tournaments, and then also, very, very esoteric questions that only Maróczy would know, and could only be validated by him. This is where a Hungarian librarian comes in, who was not told this was a case of potential survival after death. He was instead told to search for information for a biography that was being done on Géza Maróczy. Some of these esoteric questions required his family's input. Yet, later there were answers to questions that appeared wrong when given and were later proven to be right. For example, the famous one is the Romih, R-O-M-I-H, sometimes spelled slightly differently. Maróczy said, "No, I did not play that person," and the judges declared, well, he did. It turned out that Maróczy' pointed out that the name of his opponent was spelled differently (R-O-M-I). Another anomaly, related to Vera Menchik, a famous women's chess player at the time, was a question of who was linked up with a particular chess club. Even researchers did not know the answer until afterwards.

VN: So, we are talking about not only esoterica but esoteric facts that were not even known at the time. When one looks at the incredible degree of accuracy, it's very interesting. Although Eisenbeiss, and his co-author Dieter Hassler, initially published the data including a couple of supposed errors that Maróczy made, the answers 'Maróczy' gave were not necessarily wrong. For example, Maróczy had spoken about the fact that he played somebody twice in a particular tournament and effectively scored one point out of two. Now, you can get that from two draws or from one win and one loss. Ultimately, it was correct, but it was initially scored as wrong by the researchers. It was wrong only in the context of win-loss instead of draws or vice versa. This kind of subtlety is pervasive in the study.

Another time, "who came third in the tournament?" was a question. Well, you know, when you play chess tournaments, you might have won but seldom would you know who came in third place. Maróczy said, through automatic writing, one world-champion had come third when another of the world champions had come third, this kind of thing. There were really, really subtle areas of error even in the general historical data. When it came to the esoterica, there seemed to be absolutely nothing wrong with Maróczy's answers even though no one alive at the time could have given all the answers. The questions were specially composed by Eisenbeiss. He was the main author of this study and chess match that was well, well researched.

JM: I can imagine a critic would want to say that's proof it was fraud because you never get close to a hundred percent accuracy in survival or parapsychology research.

VN: Of course, one could argue both ways. When one looks at psi research amongst the living versus tests in labs, you will get nowhere near a hundred percent accuracy. You might statistically score over a thousand hits and be at the 52 percent level when you expect it to be at the 50 percent level of accuracy. The data in survival research is much higher. Of course, a survival researcher like Dr. Gary Schwartz has reported the same kind of much higher figures in survival research. But the important thing is the accuracy. Some of the responses by Maróczy later were found to be correct, yet the initial responses were scored as incorrect.

The notable points here, and this to me is the key to this whole case, are two essentials, namely both first is data and skills. Quite amazing when you put them together. The second is the most interesting: *extended* survival. The idea of survival here is not just a fragment or moment of survival, perhaps a memory or something caught in space. This was over a period of approximately six years. Strangely enough, a prediction was made that Rollans would be able to complete this experiment and he did, and then he died: another esoteric piece of information.

It is not a case of they played this chess game quickly, over a period of a few minutes: Explanations could be that "perhaps Korchnoi was fabricating, or maybe some other master was involved. Then, that person quickly consulted with Rollans and the moves were delivered to Eisenbeiss by automatic writing." The details listed make these explanations unfeasible and very unlikely. Wolfgang Eisenbeiss has been kind enough to send me all the transcripts. I have been able to view them in written format, as well.

By the way, there is a record of this study and I want to write a play about it.

His wife was interviewed, as well. Apparently, Rollans was considered a most honest individual. He performed a lot of mediumship, never accepted a penny for the work, nor had any real, let us say, financial outcome motivation. Neither did Eisenbeiss. He kept this study very, very quiet for some years.

JM: It wasn't until 2006, or 2007, that he published his analysis of the information the ostensible spirit of Maróczy provided in sessions.

VN: Eisenbeiss was encouraged to do so but, you're right. It was years later. He had no intention of really achieving great publicity out of the experiment. But oddly, there were some important outcomes to the study. In the middle of the game the press got hold of it and ran a story about the chess game. It could be argued, if this was fraud, the media were keeping a keen eye on the study throughout the second half. Korchnoi later commented, even before the end of the game, how well Maróczy was playing. In fact, he wasn't even sure if he was going to win the game. So, there were many different elements happening during the research. Later, there was another master player who examined the play beyond me: someone at a far, far higher level of chess expertise.

JM: We're talking now about the American chess Grandmaster Bobby Fischer (1943-2008) the brother-in-law of parapsychologist Russell Targ.

VN: Yes, and it was apparently through Russell that this Fischer evaluation came about, probably at Bobby Fischer's request. And of course, Bobby Fischer, some would argue, was the greatest World Chess Champion in the history of chess. Fischer might have been the greatest player in the history of chess but became extremely psychotic in his later years, as is well known. There have been movies made about his misfortune. Possibly, and again as a consequence of Russell's involvement, I understand that Bobby Fischer also went through this game—

JM: —move by move.

VN: I haven't got all the details. He went through the moves of the game because when you're playing at that level of chess, you can virtually eyeball the whole chess game and know what is going on. His comment was anyone who could give that kind of level of fight to Victor Korchnoi over that number of moves was somebody playing at the Grandmaster level. This is not my evaluation but Targ's.

JM: But you also did your own evaluation, move by move, of the match.

VN: Yes, I read the report and thought, this is very interesting. Later, I published my evaluation in the *Journal of the Society of Psychical Research,* while making comments about my strengths and weaknesses, historically, as a chess player.

JM: You do not consider yourself a chess master?

VN: No, and I gave up chess many years ago. However, I thought this study is something that needs to be sought after and reviewed. Importantly, I had a control and that was a computer. Now, computers in the late 1970s and early 1980s, are not like the chess computers today. Chess computers today— I'm afraid this is one of the last bastions of humanity: beating up on robots and artificial intelligence has failed. It has failed because chess computers today can beat even world champions. But in those days, that was not the case. I took a chess computer program that I had, and one I would regularly play: software that played at the low master level. I usually won maybe 98% of games. So, this is the kind of level it was playing. A chess program very beatable but this was the level of chess computers of the day. The question came up: maybe, just maybe all this is a fraud. The chess computers could possibly have faked this all or somebody could have faked it through the chess computers. What we found was that first the style of Maróczy— when you're at that level, in a world championship chess setting, even in 1905, you have a particular kind of style—

JM: —based on the cultural historical era.

VN: Also based on the individual player. Every player plays differently. You can recognize the games of a Bobby Fischer, somewhat. You can recognize the games of an Alexander Alekhine. You can recognize the games of Akiba Rubinstein. You can recognize the games of Nimzowitsch. In the same way, you could recognize the games of Maróczy. Stylistically it was so. I set my computer, such that, what would it respond. We were able to discover that it was pretty much impossible for the computer to have replicated this chess game between Maróczy and Korchnoi. I played the game as well, and could see it in the same kind of fabric. We were dealing with somebody who was expressing a personality structure. When you play chess weakly, you're not expressing that structure. When you play chess at that kind of level, you are. There's a style that you develop, and this was the style of Maróczy, much like we could compare the play of a Fischer but different.

JM: In addition to skill and information, you're saying the personality of Maróczy came through in the match?

VN: it came through also in some of these questions: the Romih question, the Vera Menchik question. I used the example of Fischer. There is a funny story which might illustrate the link up a little more. I had the good fortune to lecture in South Africa on the Fischer-Spassky chess series. In one of the games—one of my listeners who would listen avidly—the move would come through the radio at the time and I would say, "Fischer's next move will be X," and sure enough Fischer's next move would be X—somebody came up to me excitedly and said, it was 37 moves into the game, "You've made the same move as Bobby Fischer 35 of the 37 times." I said, "That's why I'm not Bobby Fischer," because chess is an absolute unit. When one looked at the Maróczy game, he was losing it by playing an inferior move very early on in the opening. This wasn't really his fault because that was the move that would have been played in 1905.

When he came back by playing more chess in the 1930s, for example, the alternative refutation was unknown then. When Maróczy passed, as far as I remember it was 1951. So, his move was what was known then, and it was a good move, just not the appropriate move for the 1980s.

JM: The ostensible spirit of Maróczy said he was rusty. This is a game in the 1980s—

VN: Yes, Maróczy made the comment that he was rusty—

JM: He did not keep up his chess skills in the afterlife, obviously!

VN: When we did an analysis, the thought was Maróczy was playing at the high master level; some would say the Grandmaster level. Fischer said the play was of a Grandmaster. I think it was at the high master level or even the low master level. You've got to understand that chess theory has so developed that to keep up with chess you have to keep up with the theory. It takes a long, long time to incorporate into play. People are full-time professional chess players and spend six—eight hours a day training, studying chess theories. When you prepare for a World Championship like Magnus Carlsen, the current World Chess Champion, you must be an athlete. In preparation, he lifts weights, plays a lot of table tennis, and as fit as anything because it is so stressful and difficult physically for a player in competition.

There is the physical aspect of the game and there is the absolute preparation such that I, lonely I, at this stage or when I was playing chess regularly and was keeping up with it, it is possible that I could have beaten the Maróczy of 1905. This was the case not because he wasn't much better than me, but because chess theory is such that he might have failed because of ideas that changed. Once you have a minimal advantage in chess, if you are a good chess player, you can carry through that minimal advantage and win. Even when you are playing a world chess champion, sometimes. Or you may be able to take the play to a draw but maybe not. Masters don't give up their minimal advantages either, as they are too good for that.

JM: Of course, in this match, Korchnoi did win.

VN: Yes, Korchnoi did win. This put an end to the idea that "well, if this was going to be fabricated, wouldn't it have been nice if Maróczy won?" You know, it is fascinating when you start looking at how the media talks about the game. In fact, in a Bobby Fischer movie, they talked about people with mental illness in chess and pointed to Fischer and Steinitz as examples. Steinitz, as I remember, way back in the 19th century, announced that he wanted to play God. He said he would beat God in chess. So, you go backwards in time and who was quoted, poor Korchnoi, but they didn't say he played it. The media only said there was a chess champion Grandmaster, one of the leading players in the world, who claimed to play a ghost and the media implied this was ridiculous. They made a joke about it. When you start looking at it, extended survival over a period of time is quite something. It requires one to look at all the alternative explanations.

JM: This has been a fascinating discussion of what is probably, while not a hundred percent conclusive, one of the strongest cases we have for evidence of survival after death. Thank you so much for being with me.

VN: Thank you, Jeffrey, it's my pleasure.

2

Spirit Materialization
with
Leslie Kean

⁓

Jeffrey **Mishlove** (JM): We're going to be exploring the fascinating topic of spirit materialization. My guest, Leslie Kean, is an investigative journalist. She is also the granddaughter of Robert Kean, who served ten terms as a Republican congressman from New Jersey. Her Uncle Thomas Kean was co-chair of the 911 Commission and is a former governor of New Jersey. Her early work as an investigative journalist led her to be co-author of books such as *Burma's Revolution of the Spirit: The Struggle for Democratic Freedom and Dignity,* and *Henry Hyde's Moral Universe: Where More Than Time and Space are Warped.* She began covering UFOs in 2000 with a groundbreaking story in the Boston Globe, and from then on devoted herself full time to investigating UFOs and reporting on them in the mainstream media. She was the author of the *New York Times* bestseller *UFOs: Generals, Pilots, and Government Officials Go on the Record* in 2010 and most recently, *Surviving Death: A Journalist Investigates Evidence for an Afterlife.*

We're going to be talking about one of the most controversial and, I think, exciting phenomena that has ever been reported in the field of psychical research: spirit materializations. The irony is, it's been reported repeatedly for 150 years and almost invariably people just refuse to digest it or accept it, except for a tiny handful of people who are the eyewitnesses.

Leslie Kean (LK): That's true, Jeff. I don't think most people even know the extent to which it's been scientifically documented under controlled conditions. But even so, I think there's a boggle factor: It's so hard to accept that this could happen, it's so impossible that it's just off the table for most people. When you've experienced it that changes things, but very few people ever have the opportunity of experiencing it.

JM: I know that even amongst parapsychologists there's kind of an attitude that these reports go back to the nineteenth century or early twentieth century and those people must have been deluded or something because we can't replicate it in an experimental laboratory repeatedly the way we apparently can do with card guessing experiments or remote viewing experiments. Therefore, if it can't be replicated repeatedly in the laboratory and reproduced independently by skeptical experimenters it doesn't exist.

LK: There are so many phenomena in the paranormal world that can't be reproduced in a laboratory. The thing about physical mediumship is, number one: it's very rare. There are very few people that have the ability. Number two: everything depends on what they call "energy": who is present in the room; what the circumstances are; the connection between the medium and the sitters. Bringing somebody into a laboratory and getting predictable results is difficult. But it has been done. Eusapia Palladino, a very famous physical medium, and Franek Kluski, another physical medium from Poland, were both studied in the lab. I don't think there's any reason not to respect the ability of scientists at that time to do as thorough a job as they could do now. Having studied the literature, I think they did a meticulous job in those days, particularly with these two physical mediums. It's all documented.

JM: Not to mention D.D. Home and Mina Crandon in the early twentieth century, who nearly received an award from *Scientific American* for demonstrating it in front of a scientific committee, before the famous magician Houdini stepped in. But I think another factor to consider is that when people make the claim that they can produce large scale macro-phenomena of this sort, they're almost invariably subjected to attack and, by and large, their lives are made miserable simply because they make the claim.

LK: I guess so. It just seems to be the hardest thing for people to deal with. For me personally, it is the most interesting aspect of the paranormal; the one that excites me and interests me the most is physical mediumship, which is basically PK [psychokinesis, or mind over matter] occurring to the extent that it even creates living forms and living beings. I find it so utterly astonishing and mysterious and so hard to explain that there's nothing that fascinates me more. The more impossible it is, the more I'm drawn to it. Whereas for the materialistically oriented strait-laced scientist that you're talking about, it's the opposite. The more it is that way, the more they want to get away from it. I don't understand where the curiosity is, to explore the most extraordinary phenomena that are happening on the planet. It happens in this small room in England for eight people every week. It went on and on and on, year after year and there it is. There's a whole lot of factors I think that go into why it's not interesting to people. We've talked about some of them, but I'm just astonished by that because I'm utterly fascinated by this.

JM: I think a lot of people are afraid, very simply, if it appears to their colleagues that they endorse this kind of a phenomenon. If they're not totally secure in their profession they're afraid they'll lose their job or they'll be ostracized. The social stigma for people who associate themselves with the paranormal is strong. But when it comes to macro-psychokinesis, which is one way of interpreting these phenomena, it's much stronger. Earlier you referred to Franek Kluski, a Polish medium who was researched very extensively. Let's just talk about some of that history.

LK: Franek Kluski was a Polish physical medium who lived from 1873-1943. He was highly educated, and was a playwright and a poet. He was also in the business world, a sophisticated person, and he had these abilities that seemed to run in his family. He had strange abilities as a child. First, there are a lot of materializations that took place in his seances that were very bizarre and not always pleasant to be around. There were animals and all kinds of strange creatures, and it was often chaotic in the seance room. A lot of the most respected Polish intelligentsia, scientists, philosophers and people from the Polish Society for Psychical Research sat with him, but the most important element of his mediumship is the fact that two leading scientists of the day, physiologist Charles Richet and investigator Gustav Geley—they're both French, Richet was a Nobel Prize winner—took Franek Kluski into a lab at an the Institut Métaphysique International in Paris. This was a room in which they had complete control. It had no windows. They took him in and sat with him under tightly controlled conditions. The two researchers sat on either side of the medium holding his legs and hands, so they knew he was not moving around the room. They had some light on in the room. They checked him to make sure he didn't bring anything in; all the standard things. They were astute investigators, and they knew how to employ the strictest controls so that fraud could be completely eliminated as a possibility. What these men did to document the materializations was extraordinary. They brought in a tub of hot paraffin wax, which was kept hot on top of some boiling water. They asked the materializing forms in the room to dip their hands into the wax and to make a glove around their materialized hand. Then when the wax dried the hand would dematerialize and the wax glove would drop on a table or on the lap of a sitter. This was a way of making a permanent record of these materialized hands.

There were a series of eleven successful seances at the Institute in 1920, followed by a series in Warsaw in 1921. They call them seances, it's just the word that's used to describe a sitting with a physical medium. I don't really like the word, but that's what they used. You can read the detailed descriptions written by Geley and also by others in the room. Sometimes they could see the little lights forming around the hands and they could see what was happening as they were dipped into the paraffin. They could hear the wax splashing, the wax would drip around the room, then these wax things would drop on them. Afterwards, they could take these wax gloves, pour plaster in them, remove the wax and then they would have a perfect replica of a materialized hand.

What's interesting is that if you look at these molds, the wax was so thin, paper-thin, that a hand could not remove itself from that wax without destroying it. Another interesting factor is that sometimes they were two hands with fingers interlocked. Imagine trying to slide a hand out when they're interlocked. You have them in positions with a finger pointing or something. Another evidential component was that some of them were child size. Even though they had the features of an adult hand, they were the size of a child's, which is another paranormal component that points towards the impossibility of some human being in the room having created the wax gloves. The scientists were very careful to control things and made sure everyone in the room held hands at all times. Richet and Geley would sometimes slip dye into the wax without telling anyone else in the room. They wouldn't tell anybody including the medium that they put that dye in there, and then when the molds were made, they could compare it to the actual wax in the room. They measured everything. They measured the amount of wax that was there at the beginning versus the amount at the end and how many molds were made and how much they weighed. Very meticulous.

I absolutely love these molds.[2] I remember when I discovered them during research. They were this most miraculous manifestation of the reality of materialization. I used to stare at the photographs all the time. There's a big thick book about them written by Geley in 1927, with long detailed descriptions of every single time when one was made and how it was made, and photos of both perfect and imperfect gloves and molds. I had the opportunity to go to the Institute in Paris in 2016, where these molds are stored. They're locked in a vault and kept in the dark, and rarely brought out. The curator there was nice enough to show four of them to me and allow a film crew I was with to film them. I was able to actually look at them and touch them, and that was a major moment for me. They have this kind of magical, mystical quality to me, but they're physical; they're real. To me, they are like sacred relics. They're very important evidence in my mind for the reality of this.

JM: What surprises me is that something as delicate as a paraffin glove could sustain the plaster being poured into it. I've read about these in the past and I always assumed that the hand was dipped into like a bowl of paraffin and then the bowl hardened and then the hand dematerialized and the plaster cast was made.

LK: No, the hand would dematerialize inside the wax, when the wax was cool. It was very thin, and they lost a lot of the gloves in the process because they were so delicate. There were a lot that were only partially formed. I think they were extremely careful when they slowly poured the plaster in and they perfected a technique. Then when it hardened, they would scrape the wax away. But they were able to do it for enough of them that they're well preserved.

---

2   https://www.metapsychique.org/the-kluski-hands-moulds/

JM: You write about Thomas Mann, the great German writer, who attended some of these seances and wrote very eloquent descriptions. As I recall, he described himself as becoming seasick just watching the paranormal phenomenon occurring. It was almost more than he could handle.

LK: That's right. I put it in *Surviving Death* partly because his descriptions were just so eloquent and beautifully written, in the style of writing you don't see much anymore. He described it as so shocking and disorienting that he said he felt seasick. He felt he was literally seeing something impossible. Yet there it was, and he had to reconcile that. It's shocking, and he was an intellectual. He never expected to witness anything real when he went to the séance. I think it does have a very big effect on people when they see it for the first time. And, despite the seasickness, he came back a second time for more.

JM: In the context of spiritualism, the point of these materializations is to provide proof of an afterlife and yet you've explored this with our mutual friend Stephen Braude, a very rigorous analytical philosopher, who suggests that the most extreme physical manifestations do not necessarily prove that an afterlife exists.

LK: Absolutely. That is the big question. I think we open-minded people who look at the scientific studies—rigorous reports on mediums like Palladino, Kluski, D.D. Home and Margery Crandon—we can agree that these things happened. That's irrefutable, as the data shows. The question is, how are they happening? Are they caused exclusively by human beings, which is the argument that Stephen Braude makes? Or are they caused by the spirits in the afterlife manipulating the substance of ectoplasm, which we can talk about, and coming through and creating these living forms or moving things in the room? Or, some combination of the two?

Most mediums are certain that it is the spirit world operating through them. This is their experience, and this is what the "spirits" speaking through them tell the sitters. The mediums are in trance throughout. That's another component with physical mediumship. Eusapia Palladino wasn't always in a total trance, but somebody like Franek Kluski, where you have actual physical materializations, that medium is not consciously there. I think the source of the energy causing these manifestations is a very hard thing to nail down. There's an argument to be made on either side. I find it hard to comprehend after having witnessed it myself and experienced a full-form materialization more than once and hearing the voice speak.

I find it hard at some gut level to accept that this is just something that these human beings in this room are somehow able to do, and it's just another form of PK, which is what Stephen will argue. From a rational standpoint it makes sense. He'll say there's no difference between the materialization of a finger and the materialization of a full person. It's the same process. Philosophers make rational arguments but I'm not sure this can be explained on a rational level. There's so much involved with the experience of it and I'm not saying that one becomes gullible, but there are a lot of factors at play. Stephen has never experienced anything like this. So, I don't think we can prove it one way or the other.

JM: As an investigative journalist you set out to see if you could witness this for yourself. Let's talk about that process because, for the most part, these days, even in the parapsychological community the general understanding is that physical mediums aren't available anymore. You get spoon benders and people who can do psychokinesis such as Ted Owens, about whom I wrote a book, *The PK Man*, but physical mediumship was considered largely extinct.

LK: I think it still is. I think there's some truth to that. There are also physical mediums—and there have been in the past—that do commit fraud and I want people to understand that I'm not denying that. There was a reason that they were considered to be frauds, because many of them were. Even today since I've been working on this there have been questions of fraud with certain people. There is sort of a tendency now for mediums to get trained and then in a couple of years they're out charging money for their work as they travel around the world. It's a different climate than it was in the earlier days when people had the patience and time to sit week after week, year after year, and let things unfold gradually. That doesn't really happen anymore. I've looked around a lot. I've sat with various mediums. There's only one that I would totally trust. I was fortunate enough to have spent five years sitting, studying, and trying to understand the work of this one medium. But it isn't easy to find physical mediums that have been tested, that are mature, that have fully developed, and that have a level of integrity that you can trust at all times and in all circumstances. There may be more than we realize because of the stigma associated with this. I'm sure there are mediums practicing all over the world and nobody knows about them. That's the other thing.

JM: Stewart Alexander, with whom you worked and whom you portray on your website, has a couple of videos in which he tells his life story. He makes a point of saying that even though he's worked with you, and he has written a chapter in your book, *Surviving Death*, for most of his career he didn't want publicity and even today keeps it to a real minimum. He's aware of the terrible fate of other mediums who were in the public light and who were badly mistreated because of it.

LK: That's right. He's very sensitive about that and very concerned that that's going to happen to him. Not so much now, but he's concerned about it after he's gone, about the legacy that it leaves behind for his family. He's got grandchildren he's close to, so he's always been very private. The fact that that video even exists on my website is a miracle, that he allowed that. He just wants to sit quietly week after week and he's been doing this for 40 years, which is a long time.

JM: One of the things associated with his mediumship is the production of ectoplasm, which has been documented repeatedly in different countries with different mediums for the last 150 years. You've had the opportunity to witness the production of ectoplasm. Let's talk about that.

LK: Ectoplasm is an actual substance and, as you've mentioned, it's been documented, and it's been photographed while being produced by various mediums. People can find out how to look at those photographs, but it always looks pretty weird in photographs. It's a substance that is emitted from the body of the medium. From their perspective it allows the spirit team—spirit people working with them—to use it to materialize themselves or to make rods and move things around the room. It's got a physical component to it. It's really a kind of energy substance, but you can see it. Nobody understands it. But I have seen it and so have many other people with Stewart Alexander. Another factor is a lot of his work is done in the dark and people have questions about that. "Well, if it's in the dark then you can cheat." Blah blah blah. We can discuss that too.

But the situation with ectoplasm that I've witnessed takes place with a light on it. You can see a cloud of ectoplasm coming over a table in front of Stewart that has light underneath it. It just looks like a cloud, almost like water, but it's not water. I've been able to witness it form itself into a hand right before my eyes. I've been able to touch the hand and feel that it is a solid physical human hand. It bangs on the table to let us know it's physical and then it withdraws and is gone. In that situation I was able to witness the ectoplasm as just plain ectoplasm and then actually watch it form into this physical hand that could move around. While that is happening, the spirit person whose hand it is, is speaking through the medium and explaining what's going on and directing the sitter when to touch it and how to operate because ectoplasm is very sensitive. You don't want to make any mistakes or do anything that you shouldn't do, or it can be dangerous for the medium. There are a lot of complicated factors here.

JM: One of the most fascinating aspects of all of this is that the spirit who produced a hand through the medium Stewart Alexander, with whom you work, this spirit is referred to as Walter. The spirit, Walter, was also very well known in the 1920s as the deceased brother of the medium popularly known as Margery, Mina Crandon, who was a high society lady. She was also a very famous medium in the 1920s and produced all sorts of effects ostensibly through the agency of this very same spirit, Walter. If this is the same spirit who was producing phenomena 100 years ago and is still doing it today, that would seem to be evidential of actual survival.

LK: It seems like that to me, but a skeptic could say, "Well, he says he's the same Walter, but how do we really know that?" A skeptic can always argue you don't have any proof that's the same Walter who lived a hundred years ago. Stewart was very interested in Mina Crandon because she was so severely misunderstood and unfairly treated once Houdini came in and did this whole number on her. There were some problems with some wax thumbprints and there were some things that her husband was involved in that weren't exactly above board, but she was an extraordinary medium and he was very interested in her. He studied her and that was when Walter Stinson came through. The way he describes it is he was drawn to Stewart because of his interest in his sister even though he had sworn that he would never ever do this again because he felt he utterly failed the first time. He wanted to try again to see if he could remedy the situation that had happened before. He's a very powerful presence in that room. He is the one who is responsible for the physical materializations and the movement of objects.

You're astute enough to notice that because the irony is that Stewart is always very nervous about anybody even knowing that it's the same Walter. He's afraid that people will use that to discredit him. But it's in my book; it's in his memoir; it's out there for people to look at. He says he's the same Walter and he's talked about situations from before. It seems like he knows what went on with his sister. But as for the word proof, I wouldn't say it's proof, because how can you prove it?

JM: Proof is a strong word, but I would say it's suggestive. It's very suggestive. I might also mention that I did interview another author, David Jaher, who wrote a book called *The Witch of Lime Street*, about the Margery mediumship and about the famous dispute between Margery the medium and Houdini the great magician, which was on the front page of newspapers across the United States back in the 1920s. It's a very interesting episode in the history of spiritualism. But now to move on, let's talk more about your experiences with Stewart Alexander.

LK: I'd like people to know first of all that I was very careful when I first started—when I had the opportunities to sit for the first two times with him, which I described in my book—to do all my due diligence in terms of checking out the room and making sure there was no way anybody could come in or out during the sitting: checking the chair that he sits in, the table in front of him. He is strapped to his chair with cable ties, so I brought my own cable ties to make sure they weren't tricks. I feel that I was extremely careful to make sure that everything in that room was tight and that there was nothing funny going on. Not that I expected it because he'd been practicing for so long that I think that if he were a fraud, it would have been discovered by now. He had sat many times in other locations, sometimes without any of his regular circle members present, and all the things that you would want to know about somebody that you want to be able to trust, all had happened with him. He has passed the tests. It's a little boring to go on about it, but that's all in my book.

After having a long email exchange with Stewart I had the opportunity to go over to England and sit twice with him in the spring of 2015. Those were my first two experiences, and it was life changing, to put it mildly. Over the years since then I have developed a close relationship with the members of his circle and with him. In fact, I have become a long-distance part of the circle. Even in the last three years or so I've been sitting remotely from New York through the computer and joining the seances every week that way. It's a very big part of my life. Of course, when you're remote, you can't experience the physical phenomena. But the physical aspect is just part of what Stewart feels is evidential, and he feels there are other more evidential phenomena showing survival; more than Walter showing up again. When people can communicate with their loved ones and information comes through for them that he couldn't possibly know and that no one in the room could possibly know, that's really important, too.

That's more like mental mediumship, but there's one spirit person who's responsible for that component.

These spirit voices come in and out of Stewart's body when he's in trance. There are five of them and I feel like I know them as people. They have distinct personalities, distinct voices, and distinct roles that they play in the séance. The overall purpose is, of course, to show the sitters that we survive death. They all have their various ways of making that point.

JM: I understand that the voices sometimes come through his vocal apparatus. He's actually speaking and they're using his brain, his vocal cords, his nervous system. But sometimes the voices are coming from elsewhere in the room, like through these megaphones—they're referred to as trumpets—that the spirits use. His vocal cords are not always involved.

LK: That's right. That is way more spectacular as you can imagine when that happens. There is one spirit guide who speaks only separately, and his voice comes from a different part of the room, and it has a very different quality. I've experienced that many times. On another occasion, maybe once or twice, I did experience what you described, this thing they call a trumpet, which is like a cone, a megaphone. This is the thing that levitates around the room. Sometimes while it's levitating, flying around the room, which is utterly wonderful to experience, it'll stop in midair, and a voice will speak through it. It is the most bizarre thing to experience. The time I remember the most distinctly it was right in front of me. Stewart is on the other side of the room and that voice is coming right from inside of the trumpet. Sometimes you can't quite hear what it's saying; other times you might hear a couple of words, but it is like this very otherworldly strange thing, these voices. It's called independent voice and there have been mediums over the years, many mediums, which facilitate that happening. There's one called Leslie Flint who was very famous for it. That's about all that he did, independent voice. With him you could have extended conversations with your loved ones.

With Stewart this one spirit person who does that usually can't stay for too long, can't speak for too long, but he does come through independent from the medium. It's just kind of a miraculous thing. The way he describes it is that he's creating a voice box out of the ectoplasm; he uses the ectoplasm to somehow make the structure. They describe it as projecting, sort of like they can project their thoughts somehow into it and create voices from that. Believe me, I have no idea how that works but they have some way of being able to do it. That's special when that happens.

JM: I understand you've witnessed the levitating megaphone. You've also witnessed, somehow, Stewart Alexander's arms— even though they are locked down using some sort of plastic ties that are very strong—his arms can easily be freed from the ties at the direction of the spirit Walter.

LK: Exactly. Walter calls it his matter-through-matter experiment. Stewart's locked and he has a cable tie which is around the thinnest part of his bare wrists and it's very tight. When you see a medium that has a tie up on his forearm and he's wearing a thick sweater, you can imagine that maybe he could slide out, but with Stewart it's very much the thinnest part of his arm. It's just impossible for him to slide out and you can't remove that cable tie unless you have a wire cutter. What happens is—this is in the dark by the way—the sitter will be next to Stewart and put their hand on top of that cable tie and feel that it's on Stewart's wrist on top of the chair. Walter will say, "Now just move your hand an inch to the right." At that moment Stewart's arm flies up into the air, with the sitters hand still on top of Stewart's wrist. Then Walter says, "Is that cable tie still on the arm of the chair?" The sitter takes their hand off and feels that the cable is still there locked around the chair arm. Stewart's arm has gone right through it. Then Walter will pull the looped cable tie (attached through the underside loop on the arm so it can't slide off) through the arm of the chair and give it to the sitter as a gift. I have three or four of those cable ties in my possession. They are all over the world with people who have taken them with such joy as a memento.

They need the dark to produce a lot of the phenomena. When Stewart began his development, he began it in the dark because he felt that would facilitate phenomena. When they started sitting, he just felt like things would be more likely to happen this way. Even the experimenters who have studied mediums in the light acknowledge that phenomena are more powerful and more likely to occur with less light. It's just the way it seems to work. It's especially true when you're working with ectoplasm. With the matter-through-matter experiment, they've been able to put the light on a second after his hand has come through the ties so people can see it, but not while it's going through. You can hear a snap as it goes through which Walter has said is not anything breaking. It's got something to do with the energy, the burst of energy, that's taking place at that moment. It's not something physical within the cable tie.

I took one of the cable ties to [a] scientist friend and had it looked at, with the highest resolution microscope for looking at physical materials to see the molecular structure. I just wanted to see if there was anything they could see. There was absolutely no sign of anything having disturbed the structure of the cable tie. I thought that was kind of interesting. It would have been great if there had been. I've seen it happen and so have so many other people. Anyway, a lot of people are skeptical because they'll say, "Oh, magicians can do things like that." But I think if you're in the room and you see where that cable tie is on his arm and how tightly it is locked, I think that anybody there would not be able to claim that this is a trick.

JM: This is all very sensationalistic. Obviously, it sounds unbelievable. Most people are probably going to say, whether they believe it or not, they understand it's kind of unbelievable because it's so rare. But the interesting thing to me is that it's not done for the benefit of a performance. These groups have been working together sometimes for many years. I understand from Stewart Alexander, it took him many years of sitting week after week after week with the same group of people to develop these abilities very slowly.

LK: That's right. He has incredible patience, and it was very slow. With some of the mediums in history that hasn't been the case. It's been a lot faster. When Stewart started, he didn't think that he was a medium. He was just fascinated by it, and he wanted to sit with some friends so they just sat for the enjoyment of sitting in the dark to kind of see if a spirit would come through in some way. Then gradually things started to happen to him. The experience I described of witnessing that hand materialize from ectoplasm took years of Walter working on it for Stewart to be able to facilitate it. So, each step along the way took a long time.

It's nothing about performance. Stewart went through a period where he did what he calls public demonstrations, where he felt it wasn't fair that more people didn't get to see it, so he would do larger groups maybe once a week or so. People would be able to be guests and come sit. There have been a lot of people who have been guest sitters over the years, but he really is interested in sitting quietly with his group and developing his mediumship because new things are always being developed. They're always working on what they call experiments, developing new abilities, testing new things, and that's what's meaningful about it.

JM: And now you have become a part of his group, I gather.

LK: I kind of have. I was so fascinated by it and wrote the book. Then I went back and sat more. I now sit remotely. Whenever I can go over there I do. The last time I was there was just before Covid. We have a small group here in America that sits with him every week through the computer. This is an experiment that Walter's been ecstatic about. He's absolutely thrilled to be able to play with having sitters at long distances and see if he can create phenomena in the space where we are. That was developing but we had a big interruption during the pandemic, and now it's picking up again. It is something I'm very involved with and it's something I look forward to every week. There were some very interesting things that were happening physically, in this part of the world. Of course, Walter says that time and space means nothing to him and his team; it doesn't make any difference. So this is a way that I can stay connected every week.

JM: Has it affected you personally? Has it changed you in any way?

LK: Oh, yes. I would say it expanded my perceptions tremendously. You're seeing things that are supposed to be impossible, over and over again. I feel that I'm way more accepting of the power of consciousness, the fact that consciousness is not just something locked into our brains, because regardless of whether these phenomena are caused by human consciousness or spirit, or both, it's a statement about what consciousness is capable of. It gives me a different perspective on the physical world, that there's so much more to reality than the physical world. The possibility of an afterlife is stronger, a much closer connection to recognizing that when we die, some aspect of who we are goes on to live somewhere else. I sometimes have doubts still because I'm rational about everything. But in terms of my experience of five years of this, it certainly makes me much more open, much more connected to that reality of survival. That's extremely valuable. I've witnessed so many people getting these communications from loved ones where evidence is provided. When you walk into this space, a place of love and harmony among all participating, and the seance unfolds, you really feel like you're dwelling in another world, or the meeting of two worlds. And then these miracles happen. It's indescribable. And yet the source and the mechanism which makes this happen remains just as mysterious and unknown as it is with UFOs. And somehow, they are probably related.

JM: In one instance, you write about being in the room—it was totally dark I gather—but during that session a full-bodied materialization occurred.

LK: I hope people are not turning off the interview at this point. This is unbelievable. But it happens. So, there's one spirit person who works with Stewart named Dr. Barnett. He's the same one who speaks independently that I was describing earlier. Distinguished, British, he was a doctor when he was here on Earth. He is the one spirit person who materializes fully in the seance room. It doesn't happen that often, but I've experienced it maybe three or four times in all the years I've been there. The last time I experienced that was in May of 2019. I wrote about it in my epilogue to Stewart's book. I tried to put into words what it's like to experience that, which is very difficult because it's ineffable.

What happens is, they'll tell you that this is going to happen. There's a cabinet that Stewart will go into only when this is going to happen. It's an enclosed space with a curtain around it. There are luminous bands around the curtain. Normally, he's not in that space. But when there's going to be a full-bodied materialization he and his chair go inside the cabinet, and the curtains are closed. The first time I saw this, Stewart's chair (with him strapped to it) was levitated and carried into the cabinet. It was just a few inches off the ground, and you could see it because Stewart's illuminated kneepads were visible. When Dr. Barnett comes out you can see the curtains opening because they're illuminated around the edges. Stewart is still strapped in his chair. You hear the flapping of the curtains and then Dr. Barnett will talk as he walks into the room. Sometimes you hear footsteps. He'll make the footsteps intentionally for the sitters to hear.

The last time this happened he came and stood right in front of me and put two very large hands on top of my head. He just tapped my head up and down like this. It felt odd, because it was very fast. He was talking right in front of my face. The familiar voice was there, talking from his ectoplasmic created body while he's touching my head. He said, "I just wanted you to know that I'm a solid human being." He really spent a long time with his hands on my head. To realize that this person didn't exist a few minutes ago was beyond anything the rational mind could grasp. You can't see him, but you can feel his hands and he's talking to you and then he goes back into the cabinet, and he's gone.

There have been incidents in the past where he came out of the cabinet carrying an illuminated ball of ectoplasm—other people have witnessed this—where they could actually see his hands. There have been a lot of spectacular things that happened before I ever met Stewart, and that's one of them. It is really hard to comprehend, and I don't blame people for having all kinds of thoughts about whatever they might be thinking. But I can assure you that this isn't a fake situation. It really happens.

JM: I know the autobiography of Mrs. Gladys Osborne Leonard, who was one of the great mediums from the 1930s, describes her development. As she developed her own mediumship, she sat in circles like this for months at a time without anything happening. Then eventually there came a point where a full-bodied materialization like this occurred and the spirit began dancing. You could hear the tapping of the feet and so on. But in your case, I think it's important for people to understand you're still working as an investigative journalist. You haven't lost your sense of objectivity. You're writing articles for *The New York Times*.

LK: That's true. I always keep that perspective. While I'm having the experience, I allow myself to be completely immersed in that experience. But then afterwards I've got tapes. Every session with Stewart is taped, so I have all of it on audio tape. You're right, I feel like I'm very objective about it and I trust my ability to be that way. I'm not gullible, so maybe that helps. But the other point you're making about Gladys Osborne, there have been physical mediums throughout history that have way more full-bodied materializations than Stewart does. Some of these people even worked in the light. Somebody like Alec Harris, who was probably one of the greatest materialization mediums ever; countless people described witnessing the forms walking around. Stewart has great abilities but compared to some of the giants of the past, they did a lot more of this than he does. There are a lot of great books out there, by the way. There's a book on Kluski, which is wonderful, and books about all these physical mediums and great scientific papers that have been written by people who have studied them. It's all there.

JM: You mentioned Charles Richet, who was a Nobel laureate, witnessed full-bodied materializations. Sir William Crookes, who was the president of the British Royal Scientific Society, witnessed full-bodied materializations. There's a very extensive literature on this. Well, Leslie Kean, it has been a great pleasure to have this time with you. You have a whole other book on UFOs, and you're deeply involved in an ongoing exploration of life after death. I'm excited about the possibility of further conversations with you.

LK: Thank you so much, Jeff. I really like being on your show and I love the work you do, so I'd be happy to come back any time.

JM: Thank you for being with me.

3

Integrating the Near-Death Experience
with
Eben Alexander

Jeffrey Mishlove: Today we are going to look at the near-death experience and how one integrates it into their life. With me is Dr. Eben Alexander who is the author of several books including *Proof of Heaven*, *The Map of Heaven* and, co-authored with Karen Newell, *Living in a Mindful Universe*. Dr. Alexander is a former associate professor of Neurosurgery at Harvard Medical School. Welcome, Eben.

Eben Alexander: Jeff, thanks for having me. It's great to be here.

JM: It's a pleasure to be with you. Your book *Proof of Heaven* has been a best-seller now for quite a long time. Millions of copies have been sold; people all over the world are aware of the near-death experience that you had. I'm sure the fact that you entered this experience as a materialistic neurosurgeon makes your story even more compelling. But I think what would be interesting is to look back on that experience after ten years and how you integrated it into your life.

EA: It changed everything really. I had to go back to square one in terms of my understanding of the nature of reality. As much as people might marvel that a Harvard neurosurgeon would go through a near-death experience and come back with this story, to them it may seem like, "Oh my gosh, how in the world does that kind of an event happen?" And yet for me it was simply the soul journey that one would expect. It is important to point out that near-death experiences have tremendous commonalities, which indicate that they're occurring in one very real realm. It is independent of one's prior religious beliefs, what country you grew up in, or even what millennia you live in. In addition, each NDE is tailor-made for the soul undergoing it.

Looking back on it, it's perfectly natural that for a hardcore materialist neuroscientist, like myself, who fully believed the brain creates consciousness, that I would have an NDE that would make me question the rough edges and reality around my knowledge base. It led me into a deeper understanding of something about which I've had a passionate interest my whole life, which is a deeper understanding of the nature of reality, the relationship between mind and brain, and the fundamental nature of conscious awareness itself. My NDE was tailor-made for me, but I had never read the near-death experience literature before and had no idea of the commonalities. I had always just thought of such experiences as a trick of the dying brain, so what do they matter? Having my own NDE was a mind-bender and part of the personal message. It also involved a disease that was, in many ways, a perfect model for human death.

A neuroscientist interested in understanding brain-mind and consciousness couldn't imagine anything better than a severe case of bacterial meningoencephalitis. It's a perfect model for systematically dismantling the primary engine of awareness according to modern neuroscience. The neocortex is the most powerful calculator in the human brain, and one that is, according to their view, involved with all of the detailed conscious awareness of everything we've ever experienced, that we see, that we hear, all of our thoughts, our language, rational thinking, free will, executive function and perception of our body in space—every bit of that depends on some part of the neocortex still working. My gram-negative bacterial meningitis caused damage not only of my neocortex, but of my brain stem. This was a very severe case. The CT and MRI scans revealed full thickness damage, that I had swelling all the way down to below the six layers of my neocortex to where they intersect with the white matter.

JM: In effect, it's a miracle you're alive.

EA: Let's put it this way. My doctors estimated that when I first got to that emergency room seizing and in coma on that Monday morning, November 10th of 2008, that I had a 10% chance of survival. So that's not a miracle, that's a 10% chance. By the end of the week, I was down to a 2% chance of survival.

JM: But then they never thought you would fully recover.

EA: See, that's the part that really is miraculous and that my doctors to this day would tell you is inexplicable based on Western medicine. Basically, when I woke up in the ICU bed on day seven of coma ... Waking up is not really the right word to use because all I remembered was that incredible spiritual journey I had been on. One anomaly of my experience is that I was amnesic. I didn't remember anything of Eben Alexander's life. During the entire coma experience I had no words or language at all. When I did wake up on day seven of my coma with my mother, my sisters, my former spouse, and my sons at the ICU bedside, I had no idea who these beings were: that's how wrecked my thinking was. But soon after that they extubated me: my words and language came back very quickly. Within a day or two, I was recognizing people quite readily.

The six faces that I described seeing towards the end of my near-death experience would materialize out of the muck and utter a few sounds that I couldn't interpret and then disappear again. Five of those were people who were physically present in the ICU room during the last 24 hours of my coma. There were many family and friends who had been there earlier in the week who I did not remember at all. Those five faces I saw at the very end of my conscious awareness of the experience meant that the vast majority of the coma experience happened between days one and five. My Glasgow Coma Scale, which normally ranges from three in a corpse to fifteen in a normal waking person, with any score below nine being deep coma, was between five and seven on those days. My doctors also knew from the scans that the entire neocortex was involved.

The part that is miraculous is that all of my memories came back within two months after my coma. In fact, after having conversations with family and friends over the next year or two I found that my memories came back more completely than they had been before. To me, it was a very strong indicator that memory is not even stored in the brain, which is something that we cover in detail in the third book, *Living in a Mindful Universe*. It's a shocking reality to modern neuroscientists, but neurosurgeons have suspected this for a long time. In spite of the millions of neocortical resections—removal of brain tissue—over the last century, there has never been a case where a broad swathe of identifiable long-term memories have been deleted. It doesn't appear that physical memory is stored in the brain at all but that our brain serves as an access point to both consciousness and memory.

When I first awoke, I had no idea how sick I had been. I assumed, given that it was way too real to be real, that it had to have been a vast hallucination. As I spent the next weeks and months reviewing my medical records, my scans, and talking it all over with my neurologists and other doctors, I began to realize the medical records I was reviewing were those of somebody destined to die, certainly not of someone who would have a profound experience and then come back to tell the world about it. I think my story really garnered significant interest in the scientific and medical communities, and that's why I've been asked to give talks to medical and surgical and nursing groups around the world.

JM: To my understanding, the brain of an adult human being doesn't regenerate itself. In a child I'm told the brain is very plastic.

EA: Right. That's very true. Neuroplasticity, the ability of new neurons to form and form new connections, is certainly more robust in children than in adults. I finished medical school in 1980, my residency in 1987, and back in those days we really didn't believe there was any significant neuroplasticity in adult brains. We've since discovered that is just not true and that people can manifest quite extraordinary modes of recovery. My case is one example of neuroplasticity even though it still is something that most doctors would consider miraculous. A gram-negative meningoencephalitis like I had is the worst kind you can have. My cerebral spinal fluid glucose level, which normally would be 60-80mg/dL and somebody with a very bad meningitis might go down as low as 20mg/dL, went to 1 mg/dL. None of my doctors or their consultants had ever seen a meningitis case that severe, which is why I think my doctors to this day, find my recovery astonishing.

JM: They expected, as I recall, towards the end of the coma that if you recovered at all, which was unlikely, that you would be spending the rest of your life in a nursing home.

EA: That's correct. They didn't expect any chance of my recovering mental function, or quality of life. On that seventh day of my coma, the doctors held a family conference where they said that things were not working out well. I'd been on three very powerful intravenous antibiotics and on a ventilator all week long, but my neurologic condition was not improving at all. The doctors thought it would be smarter just to let nature take its course and to stop the antibiotics. It was a few hours later that I came back to this world, but my brain initially seemed absolutely wrecked by the experience.

JM: It took months for you to really recover.

EA: It did take two months for everything to come back. For the first week or two it was very frightening for my family to witness because they thought, "Oh, this wonderful miracle, he's coming back to us, but oh my god, he's totally wrecked, this is horrible, it would have been better for him to die." That's why the doctors had recommended to stop treatment. My recovery was so extraordinary that I could even discuss and review my medical records with my doctors within a month or so, which to them was an absolute shocker.

JM: Immediately after you came out of the coma, I gather you were rather delirious.

EA: Yes, I was in fact. That's a beautiful part of the story that I share in *Proof of Heaven*. After they extubated me, I was told by my family that I was sitting on the bed like this little Buddha saying, "All is well. Don't worry. All is well." I do not remember saying those words but there were many witnesses and I'm sure I said it with utter conviction. Even though I had been extubated and they thought I was waking up, I was in and out of a wild, delusional, paranoid nightmare for about 36 hours, but I knew that that was a delusion. There were parts of it that seemed very real, and it took a little convincing from my family that it wasn't. For example, part of the delusion was that I was in a cancer hospital in south Florida that had three adjacent buildings with escalators through them. Though I can remember it now, it's kind of a foggy memory though at the time it seemed real.

JM: You were in Virginia.

EA: I was actually in Virginia. My family challenged me on how I got to Florida. I told them that I got there using a system of elaborate underground tubes and trains. But the interesting thing is how fuzzy that memory is compared to the memories from the deep coma. The spiritual journey that I reported in *Proof of Heaven* that happened when I had a documented Glasgow Coma Scale of six to seven, is as sharp and clear today as if it happened yesterday.

I've since discovered several scientific papers from American and European doctors who study NDEs. They looked at the quality of memories over time comparing a near-death experience to dreams, psychedelic drug experiences, imaginary experiences or important real-life experiences. The interesting thing that these scientists have uncovered about near-death experiences is that those memories are far more stable and resilient over time than any others. I've given more than four hundred talks to audiences around the world about my experience and I often have people coming up to me after these talks, many of whom are completely naïve to the NDE literature, and they will say, "I've never told anybody this before, but ... " and then they'll share their NDE story with me. It could have happened sixty years ago and yet they claim to remember it as clearly as if it just happened yesterday. These stories are very extraordinary and are not hallucinations nor dreams and they were not the effect of psychotomimetic drugs.

There was a non-medical press article about my case that was completely erroneous and misinterpreted many facts about my coma and the associated medical treatment. It was basically an *ad hominem* attack stating that I was in a coma due to pharmacologic manipulation. My records state that I was in a deep coma from the moment that I was taken by the EMTs from my home, long before any IVs or drugs were used, and I stayed in that coma all week long. I was still on very heavy sedation when I came out of the coma. A case report authored by Bruce Grayson and his co-investigators at UVA came out in the *Journal of Nervous and Mental Diseases* in September of 2018, making a very clear case that I was in a deep coma due to severe brain damage from meningitis. The reason that's important to the medical community is because the destruction of the neocortex should get rid of any hallucination, dream, or drug effect of conscious awareness.

JM: One of the unique features that you described that I haven't encountered in other accounts of near-death experience is that when you first arrived in this alternative reality you found yourself embedded in an unpleasant muck.

EA: It sounds foreboding and kind of unpleasant but given that I was totally amnesic, it was like my birth into the universe as pure awareness. I had no memories of Earth or humanity or being Eben Alexander. None of the words or language, religious concepts, or scientific knowledge, made it through. That *tabula rasa* or empty slate was very important for the journey I had to go through which only became clear months and years later. That was part of the teaching about the brain-mind connection and the nature of consciousness, that I had to delete all of my memories. Then of course they came back even better than they were before in the two months after the coma. It all started with, what I call, the earthworm's eye view, like being in dirty jello. Even though I had no body awareness during any part of the journey, I was aware and could sense around me. I remember roots or blood vessels everywhere. Given that I had no memory moment-to-moment it seemed to go for eons. But it didn't; it ended because I became aware of this slowly spinning very clear white light that had fine silvery and golden tendrils flowing off of it. As that white light came towards me, one of the most beautiful aspects of it is it came through associated with a perfect musical melody, the notes of which proved crucial. Human beings have used sound for tens of thousands of years to get into altered states of conscious awareness. For example, the didgeridoo, which I think is one of the most healing musical instruments on earth, supposedly has been around for 40,000 years. Sound, vibration, frequency not only removes us from the four-dimensional space-time of this very dense material realm to help liberate our conscious awareness, but it also serves as a vehicle used to traverse multiple spiritual realms.

That spinning melody of light ushered me up from that earthworm's eye view into this beautiful gateway valley that in many ways seemed much more real than this world. It had beautiful, lush plant growth everywhere, all of it growing very dynamically. There were no signs of death or decay anywhere. I remember sparkling blue waterfalls flowing into these crystal blue pools. There were thousands of beings down below us all dancing. When I came back to this world and tried to put words to it, I labeled those beings as souls between lives. They were dressed in very simple peasant garb made of beautiful colors beyond the rainbow. There was lots of joy and merriment going on, with children playing and dogs jumping, incredible festivities down below.

I was a speck of awareness on a butterfly wing where millions of other butterflies were looping and spiraling in these vast formations. Up above were these swooping, golden orbs of light, each one a pure spiritual essence and they were leaving these sparkling golden trails against this blue-black velvety sky. The entire scene was lit by these billowing clouds of pure color. These swooping orbs up above were emanating chants, anthems, and hymns that would thunder through my awareness and resonate this incredible power of oneness, of identification. It's one of the reasons why it's so difficult to explain these journeys because we're not seeing with the eyes or hearing with the ears which are filtered by the brain and are thus limited sensory modalities. In these spiritual realms we essentially see through everything because we are becoming huge swathes of the entire scene and forming this beautiful model of all of it that transcends four-dimensional space-time. It's an extremely elaborate form of knowing.

JM: It's amazing you can put it into words at all.

EA: I struggled with the words for *Proof of Heaven* trying to get it right. At the end of the day, I finally felt like the words were about as good as I could muster. I often feel that way when I'm giving presentations, interviews, and conferences. But you're absolutely right: you cannot put it into words. That's one of the reasons why I think people confuse it with a dimethyltryptamine (i.e., DMT) trip, which is a hallucinogen that purportedly is found in minute amounts in human beings although that is up for debate. Though the descriptive words may sound the same, they are not describing the fullness of the journey. This is much more involved than a psychedelic drug trip in terms of its reality and meaning. The scientific literature finds that all the transcendental aspects of a near-death experience, like encountering souls of departed loved ones, full-blown oneness with the power of pure love at the creative source of the universe, and life mission and seeing one's future, aren't as readily apparent in a psychedelic drug trip.

JM: There was also a timeless quality, like you might have been there for years.

EA: It actually triggered a tremendous interest I have regarding the nature of time. The one thing that became very clear to me is that what we see as past, present, future is very much a fiction. When you get into conventional science, whether you're talking about the Theory of Relativity and how spacetime works relative to gravity, or you look at the quantum physics findings that time can flow in loops, the only thing that gives us a forward sense of time in our human macro sized world is the Second Law of Thermodynamics, which deals with the entropy of particles. But, other than that Law of Thermodynamics, time should easily flow both directions and yet we have this sense that it only goes in one direction.

In my journey, I had to label it something that I call "deep time." I've heard the phrase used by others in slightly different ways, but I think all of us are trying to converge on the notion. For me, deep time is a completely different ordering of causality that you have to invoke when connecting to those realms. For example, that gateway valley was only a steppingstone on my way out. That would be the same realm where we go through life reviews and reunite with our higher soul at the time of leaving the physical body. The life review is very important. It's been described by near-death experiencers going back at least 2,400 years. Plato wrote about the Armenian soldier, Er, killed in battle.

He was dead on the battlefield for several days before they finally collected all the bodies and put his on a funeral pyre. Just before they lit it, Er came back to life. The journey he portrayed is that when you die you go through a review of the most important and pertinent lessons of your life still to be learned. If you're one of those who handed out pain and suffering to others as soldiers often do, you've got to be ready to face that. We reap what we sow. In essence, the life review is a beautiful example of how the boundaries of self are a fiction. They support the drama of this world where we have apparent separation of self from other self. In a life review you experience the impact not only of your actions but even your thoughts on those around you, and you experience it as they experience it. That's why it's such a good course corrective for us to learn how to treat others.

JM: This was part of your experience.

EA: It was part of the experience. That's why we should treat others as we would like to be treated. It appears as a neutral ground even though, in that life review setting, it's in that infinite ocean of pure unconditional love of that god force. So many near-death experiencers bring that experience back to this world and know full well in their own heart, that there's nothing to fear about death. It's a reuniting with that ocean of absolute warmth, love, kindness, compassion and mercy of that creative source of this universe.

JM: You are experiencing the pain and joy that you are responsible for in other people but experiencing it through their eyes, their feelings.

EA: Their feelings. Their heart. That's a good reason to remember to treat others as we would like to be treated.

JM: It also suggests that at some level of our consciousness we are everyone.

EA: We are, absolutely. I think that is something that we make a very clear point of in our third book, *Living in a Mindful*

Universe. It was clear to me in my coma journey that we're really sharing one mind, that when we die it's basically like a raindrop falling back into the ocean, in a sense. Although there's this tremendous body of evidence concerning reincarnation and scientific study of reincarnation. So it's really not a question of whether or not you want to believe it or if your religious texts support it, most religious texts do. In fact, original Christianity fully supports reincarnation. Christ talking about the prophet who was reincarnated as John the Baptist. But it was actually Constantine several centuries later who made any talk of reincarnation punishable by inverted crucifixion. He didn't like that idea because of how it interfered with their ability to control people with what they were putting together at the Council of Nicaea and that kind of thing, codifying and unifying Christian religious thought. But certainly, reincarnation is completely compatible with early Christianity and other phases. And then you have the scientific evidence that supports it today. For any of your listeners who are interested I would steer them to UVADOPS.org, which is the Division of Perceptual Studies at the University of Virginia under the guidance initially of Ian Stevenson back in the 60s, 70s, 80s; more recently of Dr. Jim Tucker. They've studied more than 2700 such cases of past-life memories in children.

JM: Let me ask you this question because you spent your whole life as a materialistic scientist. You've had this incredible experience but you also have a lifetime of habits of thinking differently. It must have taken you a while to absorb all of this to come to the realizations that you now have. They didn't happen overnight.

EA: It didn't, you're right. I had to question everything going back to the very beginning which includes any of the assumptions I had about the nature of reality. One of the most fundamental assumptions in conventional materialist neuroscience is that only the physical world exists. If only the physical world exists then you've got to come up with a way to explain consciousness and mind based on the physical workings of the brain. That's where it hits an absolute wall. Back in the mid-1990s David Chalmers wrote his book, *The Conscious Mind*, which was a consolidation of several decades of work from around the world that were pointing out that the workings of the brain do not explain the workings of the mind. In fact, I very much revere the work of a Canadian named Wilder Penfield who was one of the most renowned neurosurgeons of the 20th century. He was in a better position than just about anybody on earth to comment on the brain-mind connection because a lot of his work involved electrically stimulating the brain in awake patients.

JM: He was a neurosurgeon like yourself.

EA: A neurosurgeon who dealt with epilepsy, one of his big topics. To resect the part of the brain that causes the epilepsy often you have to map it out. It turns out the brain feels no pain at all. I've done several hundred of those cases myself, awake craniotomies in patients where you map out the brain by electrically stimulating it and then having the patient report to you what kind of memory or sensation they are having. Initially, Penfield thought he was hot on the trail of uncovering the source of memory. He came to realize even if he resected a part of the brain that he thought contained the memory, that that memory would still be very robust in that patient. So he realized it wasn't so simple.

In fact, he wrote a book in 1975 called *The Mystery of the Mind* that summarized his work experiences. In that book he makes it clear that you cannot explain mind and consciousness based simply on the workings of the brain. You would never find anything resembling consciousness and free will in the brain and he eliminated the possibility that memory seemed to be in the neocortex.

JM: But generally, the profession as much as they revere Wilder Penfield, they didn't follow him that far.

EA: It's a real tragedy. We actually met one of his medical team in Montreal who had been involved in his medical care who said that when he published that book it was a year before he died of cancer. The story on the streets at the Montreal Neurological Institute was that the cancer had influenced his thinking, so it was a cheap cop-out. Anybody who reads the book will realize his thinking was not at all impaired. It's a very insightful and reflective book. I've read a lot of his other work around that time, the foundational work from the 1940s and 50s and his scientific papers that led to those conclusions. He was very clear of mind and couldn't have been clearer on an interpretation of the data. Yet the world, the scientific world in particular, was not ready to hear in 1975 that the brain was not the producer of consciousness.

JM: You got trained as a neurosurgeon after that. You had no problem, I imagine, assuming that consciousness was a product of the brain.

EA: That's what I was taught and that's what I believed. If we were to take that supposition and go to a modern neuroscientist or philosopher of mind and ask them if the brain produces consciousness, they won't have anything to say. There are some vague theoretical models that talk about information processing and information ordering and make some big assumptions about how that might somehow work in the brain. But in terms of actually having any notion whatsoever about how the hundred billion neurons in the brain interact to give rise to consciousness, nobody has the remotest clue.

JM: I have heard speculation about neural loops and cybernetic feedback loops within the nervous system. It's about as close as I've ever heard.

EA: They have some working models that seem to be okay at their very primitive level. Those models involve the neocortex as the main calculator, which is by far the most powerful calculator in the brain. It's amazing how those six cell layers in the neocortex have been modified to do so many functions like controlling vision, hearing, and our body position in space. Every bit of what we sense is actually an internal construct within our mind that we think is a fairly faithful model of reality. You can show, for example, mismatches between visual and tactile stimuli, by fooling that system into thinking certain things. Where we really run into a wall is with quantum physics itself. The world of quantum physics offers the most fundamental way of asking the brain-mind question implying the fundamental nature of consciousness. We explain it in pretty full detail in that third book, *Living in a Mindful Universe*. It's that much deeper kind of understanding that was forced on me.

It's really one of the biggest smoke-and-mirrors tricks of the 20th and early 21st century that modern science and especially neuroscience claim that they're almost on the verge of describing consciousness. Instead, they're on the verge of describing exactly how the brain is *not* the producer of consciousness at all, but that consciousness is something far more fundamental. This finding fully opens the door not only to the reality of the afterlife but of reincarnation. We need a much bigger theater of operations to really understand where all this is headed. The general models you're referring to would involve the neocortex as the final calculator and its interactions of the neocortex with the thalamus which are the deep gray structures, but still an advanced part of the brain. The thalamus has been found in animals going back at least a hundred million years.

JM: It's the mammalian brain, basically.

EA: The mammalian brain, exactly. But it turns out that modern neuroscience would involve deeper more primitive structures going down into the brainstem that actually play a role in igniting and unifying consciousness.

JM: I'm interested in not just the intellectual integration that you've obviously been engaged in as a professor, but what it meant for you emotionally and spiritually, to change your life so completely as a result of this experience.

EA: I put it in *Proof of Heaven*, one of the deepest scientific truths of my journey to me, when I came back from my coma and began interpreting the experience, was that ultimate healing power of love. If you try as a scientist to keep this in a very cognitive intellectual setting when you've been there and touched that and dipped into it and felt the power of it and what you hear, you cannot deny the emotional, heartfelt, loving nature of the journey. I've come to realize much more fully how all the physical, mental, and emotional aspects of each and every one of us depends ultimately on the spiritual aspects. That's what this discussion is about, consciousness in general, relationship of brain and mind, the very existence of the soul. You cannot get away from that concept of love and of the oneness of mind, which I think is one of the most important concepts.

To your interested readers, I would recommend a book by Dr. Larry Dossey titled *One Mind*, which is incredibly powerful. It's a topic he took on because, as an identical twin, he had a telepathic connection with his brother. Anybody who studies twins knows that telepathy is easily demonstrable in twin populations but what most people don't realize is telepathy is found in other people and there are ways to enhance telepathic skills. Telepathy can be more powerful when you invoke heart consciousness and emotional power. Telepathic connection to cognitive constructs doesn't have the same kind of weight and resonant power that can be found in emotional constructs. That's why telepathy and empathy often work hand in hand and there are stronger interconnections. In some of the twin studies, their connection is so strong that, for example, one twin might burn his finger on a stove and the other twin a thousand miles away develops the blister. It's astonishing. People need to realize this connection goes very deep, and it's much more than just a subtle mental connection. It can be a very powerful physical connection too in a sense.

JM: Did you regard yourself as an atheist prior to that experience?

EA: I had grown up in a Methodist Church in North Carolina. My adoptive father was an academic neurosurgeon, a beautiful mentor, a resource, and a role model. He had been a combat surgeon in the Second World War and I think he got through that conflict relatively unscathed because of his religious beliefs. He came back to be a chairman of a neurosurgical training program in the US which never conflicted at all with his faith in God. He had a very profound sense of the reality of God, the power of prayer, and yet he was also extremely scientific. He easily discussed the Big Bang, evolution, and neuroscientific concepts. Going to that Methodist Church, I remember thinking I was so smart because I knew science was the pathway to truth. Even in sixth grade I got into some lively discussions with my church confirmation teacher concerning scientific models of the origin of the universe.

I went into my early career wanting to believe what I learned in church. I had greater and greater difficulty coming up with any model of how conscious awareness could survive the death of the brain and body. As I tell the story in the book *Proof of Heaven*, in the year 2000 my faith had a tremendous shaking because I had reached out to the children's home in North Carolina back in my teens and 20s looking for my birth mother thinking she might be out there. They kept saying to me, "No, she's not looking for you. Forget about it." So fine, I'd been adopted into a loving family and they'd honored all my hopes and dreams. I could go with that.

That's the way I left it until decades later when my oldest son, Eben the fourth, was in sixth grade at Charles River School in Dover, Massachusetts and had a school project to complete a family genealogy. He said, "We have to find out more about your birth family." So, he encouraged me to write another letter to the children's home, which I did, fully expecting to get the same answer I'd always gotten before. This time I got a different answer. In a two-minute phone conversation with a social worker I found out that my birth parents had actually gotten married. Not only that but they had three children.

Their youngest child, my sister, had died two years earlier, that would have been in 1998. They were still grieving her loss, so it was not a good time to come back in their life. I didn't realize it until months later, but that phone call sent me into a dark night of the soul. I stopped taking my sons to church and saying prayers with them at night. I just gave up on my faith and became agnostic. There was no way that I saw evidence that prayer was real, that there was a loving personal God out there. I just dropped it all until my near-death experience. My coma showed me very clearly how that was all totally wrong.

JM: Because in your near-death experience there was a portion of it even above that beautiful verdant valley with the butterflies and the music where you felt you were in direct communion with the creator of the universe.

EA: Yes, that's a beautiful part of the story. I have to take us back to being on that butterfly wing with the millions of butterflies looping and spiraling above this valley. It was ultra-real, much more real than anything I've ever experienced in the material realm. That's the hard part for people to get, though more than half of NDErs talk about how much more real that realm is than this one. I wasn't alone on the butterfly wing, there was also a beautiful young woman. I'll never forget her appearance. She was dressed in the same kind of simple peasant garb that the dancers in the valley were dressed in, but with lovely colors. I'll never forget her sparkling blue eyes, her high cheekbones, high forehead, broad smile, soft light brown hair. She never said a word to me, but she didn't have to. She looked at me with a look of pure love.

I remember, around the same time that I was aware of her presence, there was this soft summer breeze that blew through the valley. Even though the scene looked the same, the breeze changed everything, like a divine wind or the breath of God. That was my first kind of knowing of the divine, given that I was amnesic for everything, I was learning about these realms for the first time. That was my first awareness of the power of that divine force of love, that God force in creating every bit of it, even the lower four-dimensional space-time that I knew was down below the spiritual realm where we'd have life reviews and all of that. But that soft summer breeze was that divine wind.

What happened next was the most stunning. Swooping orbs of angelic choirs above provided portals to higher and higher levels of awareness all the way out to what I call the core. The process of getting there was witnessing not only four-dimensional space-time collapsing down but several layers of deep time, spiritual organization, and causality all collapsing down into the core. I often use an analogy of it being like on the very edge of the event horizon of a black hole, where you're oscillating between pure absolute oneness-infinity-eternity-love-God force and the first stages of parcellation. The highest spiritual realms start to split out into a separation of that God force. In that core realm the whole higher dimensional multiverse had been compressed into what I call the over-sphere.

Even though all of eternity and infinity could be represented as this little ball, there was still beyond that infinite dimensionality overflowing with pure wholeness of love of the creator. "Creation" is the best word I can use to describe it. There was a brilliant light acting as this interpreter, or translator. But at times, because of that same oscillation on the event horizon, I was with every bit of the oneness. I think one of the biggest travesties of some of our religious orthodoxies is that they say that we cannot be one with God. They look at the human ego as such a small thing so how can that possibly be on the same terms as that infinite eternal god force? Our speck of awareness as a conscious being is a very direct link to that god force of pure oneness. The petty little ego, the linguistic rational brain and all the little meanderings of humans are way down below that. Developing that sense of the observer within is important because that awareness is something that goes all the way to that pure, self-aware core of the universe.

We are all truly one with the divine and it's what gives us the power to rise above this myth of sinfulness and bad boy behavior which is taken as an assumption. That's not who we truly are at our deepest sense of awareness, but we are in fact one with that god force. I saw that there was no battle between good and evil. There's no doubt that darkness and evil happen to people in this world but what I saw is that unconditional love has infinite power to overwhelm it. Apparent darkness and evil are only the absence of light and love. Any one of us can choose to develop that oneness with the infinitely loving God and can therefore choose to love ourselves most fully. That was another realization of my journey. The problem is not that we don't love our neighbors or our enemies enough, it's that we fundamentally don't love ourselves as those divine eternal sacred godlike beings that we can all find in deep meditation. By going through life reviews, we can come to realize what we have within us. I came to see the darkness, illness and injury we endure as providing steppingstones. It's how we deal with those things that allow us to grow.

JM: Even though this experience for you occurred 10 years ago I'm under the impression as you're recounting it it's still very much alive.

EA: It is alive. That's another misunderstanding about near-death experiences. People think you have an NDE then you come back with all the answers. You might come back with better questions and certainly better questions lead us towards better answers, but it is a mission in progress. My understanding now is that reincarnation is absolutely a real part of the picture. I know that we do this kind of work through multiple lifetimes. "Learn as if to live forever and live as if to die tomorrow," is a perfect guide because a lot of the knowledge remains with us even though there is a system of what I call "programmed forgetting." That's easily demonstrable, for instance, in all those cases of past life memories in children which is indicative of reincarnation.

Jim Tucker and Ian Stephenson would tell you to ask children questions about their past lives between ages 2 and 6. After age

6 there are multiple natural processes that build up the veil so that we forget the time between lives. We tend to forget past lives even though transpersonal psychology, thanks to brilliant investigators like Stan Grof, Michael Newton, and Brian Weiss, shows us that you can best deal with the hardships in this lifetime by realizing that the stage for them was set in other lifetimes. If you look at yourself as a multi-incarnated being, then you can get at the root cause of so many of life's difficulties. Any of the things that were not resolved in a previous lifetime nor resolved during a life review are fair game for challenges and hardships that you'll have to deal with and resolve in this (or a future) lifetime.

It's another very good reason never to succumb to suicide. Suicide is not the correct answer except in very occasional cases of euthanasia to alleviate suffering due to a terminal disease. Otherwise, suicide just postpones having to deal with those particular issues. If you can't handle them in the life review, then you have to handle them in the next incarnation.

JM: You have to deal with difficulties in any case.

EA: Yeah, there is "no way out but through." We have to deal with the stuff that we came here to deal with. The word "healing" comes from the same word as "whole" or "wholeness and health." We're all here in the process of healing to become more of who we came to this world to be. It was Socrates who said, "The unexamined life is not worth living." It really is worth reflecting on who we are, why we're here, where this is headed, what our purpose is. The greatest value to the individual for the kind of awakening we're talking about in *Proof of Heaven, The Map of Heaven,* and especially *Living in a Mindful Universe* is absolutely upon us. It does involve the entire scientific community in a paradigm shift of our entire civilization.

The real power of this message is how the individual can take it and run with it because it's all about free will. Free will is that $64 million dollar question because modern materialist science would try and convince you we don't even have free will. They'd be saying that it's all chemical reactions, electron fluxes in the brain, natural laws of physics, chemistry, biology, so where would you even insert free will? My journey showed me very clearly that the whole universe exists to support the free will decisions of sentient beings who are temporarily dumbed down to their knowledge of the grand picture. Our higher soul is between lives so that we have the emotional buy-in to live these lives, feel the pain of loss and love but also feel the glories of love and an embodiment of that divine essence of this universe and our ability to participate in it. Those are all gifts.

JM: Dr. Eben Alexander, what a delightful journey that you are sharing with people. You're a scientist and a prophet.

EA: I would say I'm just an interested open-minded guy just like any of us out there who wants to find these things out. That's why I often stress with people, you don't need to have an NDE to know all of this. To be a conscious sentient being, simply develop a method of meditation. I try to meditate an hour or two a day. I've been doing that for the last eight years or so. It gives tremendous benefits for creativity, guidance, insight, connection, relationships, and even connecting with souls of departed loved ones. It also gives us a much grander sense of who we are and what we're here to do. That kind of insight I think is absolutely of extreme value especially in this world where we live with all the social media, all the fake news, and conspiracy theories. There's a lot of nonsense out there. Going within and focusing on that heart consciousness and our inner awareness, then we find that going within consciousness is actually a way of getting out into this universe. It's a tremendous gift and all of us can avail of it and that's something that we like to share on EbenAlexander.com. People can find a lot more information about me and about this pathway of discovery.

JM: Thank you so much for being with me.

EA: Jeff, thanks so much for having me. It's been great talking with you.

4

The Spiritualist Vision of the Afterlife
with
Stafford Betty

⌒

Jeffrey Mishlove: Today we are going to explore the nature of the afterlife. With me is Dr. Stafford Betty, a philosopher and professor of religious studies at California State University in Bakersfield. Stafford is author of *The Afterlife Unveiled* and *Heaven and Hell Unveiled*, as well as a novel, *The Imprisoned Splendor,* based on a description of the afterlife, and a philosophical treatise, *Vadiraja's Refutation of Sankara's Non-Dualism.*

When we think about the afterlife there are many lines of evidence one could point to: near-death experiences, mediumistic communications, and religious doctrines. How do you approach it?

Stafford Betty: I am more attracted to mediumistic communications. I look at the scriptures of the world's religions, and I think of them not as coming from some higher plane, through some sort of godly realm; I just don't see them that way. They all seem man-made to me. What they have to say about the world beyond differs considerably one from another. I am looking for better evidence, something that's more plausible, something I can rely on more. I find that especially by looking at the near-death experience and by looking at mediumistic communications from the other side. It seems to me that what comes forth from these kinds of evidence seems more plausible, certainly more inspiring, and something I want to share with the world. That's why I write these books.

JM: Psychical researchers have been studying mediums and mediumistic communication going back to about the 1850s. We have over 150 years of research now, although, I think there's still a lot of disagreement amongst the researchers themselves as to how reliable this material is.

SB: Yes, there is. I think that the deeper one goes into the subject the more reliable it's going to seem. I'm one of the persons who has gone most deeply into the subject. What I've done is to analyze and bring together dozens of communications from the other side that purport to describe the world in which they live. I find this a lot more believable and plausible than a scripture which purports to tell us what is there but is not written by somebody who's actually there. I want a witness who can speak to me with more authority and that's what we're getting.

JM: I get the sense that some of these scriptures are written for the purpose of getting people to behave.

SB: Right. There isn't that kind of orientation among our spirit communicators. What comes through them is that they think that materialists have made a mistake. There is something on the other side, and our spirit friends want to tell the world about it. They think it's a mistake in every sense to try to navigate through life without the expectation, consolation, and hope that there is more to life than just this one life here.

JM: A skeptic would typically counter by saying that, well, of course people wish for an afterlife, and, therefore, all these descriptions are ultimately the product of a sort of wish fulfillment.

SB: Yes. This is where you have to begin to look for evidence. What is there about these communications that makes you think they are legitimate rather than just maybe subconscious wish fulfillment on the part of the medium? It could well be that all this material is coming from the medium's subconscious imagination. That is a possibility, but I don't think it's a very likely one. The reason—actually there are several—but the main one is that many communications have told us a great deal about the memories of a deceased person that can be checked. Memories that the medium knows nothing about but that the person who is alleged to be coming through would be expected to know because he or she is describing his or her life as it is remembered. Are the memories factual? In the best instances, they are impressively factual. In the very best, dozens of highly specific accounts have been matched with what friends who knew them well remember about them. In some instances, you'll even find descriptions of where a forgotten will was placed in a book in the library of the deceased person. How is the medium going to know about that information? It checks out. There is the will. There have been book tests. There have been cross correspondences: ways to check a medium's authenticity. The more you investigate this material the more likely you're going to be convinced.

JM: I recall reading an issue of the magazine of the Smithsonian Institute of 1903 surveying at that time, over a hundred years ago, the literature for psychical research on survival after death. They concluded that we're not a hundred percent sure about survival but if nothing else this literature conclusively establishes the existence of extrasensory perception.

SB: Let me tell you this, Jeff. I think this is really going way out on a limb but it's possible that, in the case that I just described, the medium would somehow have the super ESP ability to know exactly where that will was located in that particular book in that man's library. That would be a degree of clairvoyance that is harder for me to believe than the more plausible theory that it's somebody's memory who's coming through and we would expect him to know where the will was.

JM: In either case, you're dealing with some level of paranormal phenomena that suggests that we need to take a deeper look at nature. But let's assume for the moment, as a working hypothesis, that the spiritualist literature from the great mediums, at least the best of it, is authentic. Then the interesting question is, if they're describing the afterlife, what are the commonalities, what are the patterns, what is the afterlife really like, at least according to them? It would be worth it, I think even for people who don't accept the legitimacy of this literature might like to know what it is they're saying, in any case, before they reject it.

SB: They might even be attracted to it because the world that is described, the world that we will be entering at death, doesn't exist way out on one of the rings of Saturn, but is right around us. When I first came across that claim I was rather astounded because we obviously don't see anything of this world. Most of us don't have the ability to. The spirits can see us, but we can't see them. We share a common space.

JM: There are clairvoyants who claim they can see.

SB: Yes. I've had clairvoyant women—they've all been women—in my classes who tell me matter of factly, "Yes, Dr. Betty, I can see spirits." They kind of come up and tell me on the side privately. They don't want anybody else in the class to know that they have these talents. I've talked to several people who have this ability. Apparently the world of spirit interpenetrates ours. But it goes outward. It is as if the world, or our earth, is the core of this space. When you look upward to heaven, you're doing something that really is rather correct because these worlds of spirit go outward from the center, which is our earth, and the higher you go the more advanced, the more evolved are the realms; the more light filled, the more indescribable they become with the languages of earth.

JM: When you say the higher they go you don't mean in physical distance from the Earth, do you?

SB: Maybe. I'm not sure but it seems that way. The spirits speak of higher spheres. Now, what do you mean by higher? Are we to take that literally? We don't have to. But there is the reference to higher, more evolved spheres, where more advanced souls go.

JM: We use the term astral plane. In my understanding the astral plane is sort of a medieval notion. It comes from a time when it was believed that each of the planets of astronomy represented almost a glass sphere that encircled the earth, that there were these seven spheres, and the earth was at the center. Of course, that's a cosmology that's been refuted by science but has remained in spiritual traditions to the extent that we still call it the astral plane.

SB: Yes. If in fact we are sharing space with the deceased, what can we say? This is a common description. The closer you are to earth the less evolved you are. What follows from that is that as you move away from being an earthbound soul—stuck in your old patterns, stuck in your alcoholism, stuck in whatever your addiction is—as you move away from those kinds of habits, do you move upward and outward? That's the way it seems as I read this literature. But I don't want to insist on it.

JM: After all, it might be some sort of higher dimensional space in which the parameter we're talking about is not up or down as we think of it in physical space.

SB: Thank you very much, Jeff. That's consistent with what they say. That's another way to look at it. That brings us to what the world that they describe is like. First, there is an impressive though imperfect uniformity in these accounts. It's not as if you're getting a picture of some Chinese version of an afterlife, then, you get another Hindu version of an afterlife, and you get another Muslim version. You're getting the same basic picture from these various sources, from these various communicators, which leads me to believe that it's not likely that we're dealing with hallucination. I can't rule out that possibility but it's not likely. It seems to me that because they are describing something the same way, they are in contact with a reality that they all share. That world is of great interest to me and should be to any normally curious person.

JM: Why? Why should we care?

SB: First, if we believe that our life here is the only one we'll ever know, that casts a kind of gloom over what death means. We look at death, and we think, oh, we cease to exist. Most people don't like the idea of ceasing to exist. I certainly don't. If we can find evidence that there is more to life than just this planetary life, and we see it described in an attractive and plausible way, that determines how we feel about death. And that has a lot to do with how we feel about our lives. So, I am very happy to describe in my books what these spirits are telling us.

JM: I know you have about 50 different descriptors.

SB: The "nifty fifty," right. Where would you like me to start?

JM: How about at the moment of death?

SB: At the moment of death, you will find yourself gravitating quite naturally, without any effort on your part, to a sector of the afterworld where spirits of like development and like mind dwell. If you are a Roman Catholic, say a very conservative Roman Catholic, you're going to find yourself gravitating to people who in this life were conservative Roman Catholics. They will embrace you and take you in. You'll be one of them, and you'll be comfortable. That's where it will begin. There are many, many sectors. You'll gravitate not only to the proper sector horizontally; you will gravitate also to the proper sector vertically. Now we're talking about dark realms at the bottom and light-filled realms at the very top. Depending on your karma, depending on the kind of being you have formed yourself into by the choices you've habitually made, that will determine where your afterlife starts. Horizontally, it starts according to the sector. Then vertically, what matters is the kind of human being you are. If you are a selfish cruel person, you're not going to find yourself comfortable in higher environment. You're going to find yourself comfortable among people who are like you in a darker realm. These realms are described in detail by all these communicators. But they are never described as hell without ending. They are hellish, yes. But they are places one can move out of, and there's plenty of help to anyone who wants to move out. There are people from the light—from the heavenly realms—who are willing to go down and serve in any way they can. One of the ways to serve is to help these people out of their ignorance and misery.

JM: Do you have the converse? Do you have beings move from the dark realm who try to reach up to the lighter realms and pull others down?

SB: They can't. But they can reach earth, and they do. There are many descriptions in this literature of the earthbound spirit. For example, the alcoholic spirit, who dies an alcoholic and finds himself thinking of the booze and liquor that he's missing desperately because he still is an addicted being. He still loves liquor. Nothing happens just because he dies. He wants liquor. He gravitates quite naturally back to earth and finds himself in a bar in San Francisco and latches onto a guy drinking gin. So, this spirit attaches itself and tries to drink and enjoy the gin through the living person to whom he's attached. This is one way that we can be undone by spiritual presences.

JM: These are what are known as earthbound spirits.

SB: Yes. But there is another kind, and these are the truly demonic spirits. Their mission is to make as much misery for us as they can. That gives them joy. That's what gives them a sense of success.

JM: I see. In acknowledging the existence of the demonic, it seems there's some overlap between the teachings that come through spirit mediums and traditional religious theology.

SB: That is true. You find countless references to the demonic in Hinduism. You find demons, of course, in Christianity. You find these demonic spirits in all the great religious traditions.

JM: But in other regards there are many differences between theology and spiritual teachings.

SB: Great differences. For example, the conviction that some people have, particularly Protestant Christians, that what saves you is acquiescence in a formula: "I take Jesus as my lord and savior." Catholics place more emphasis on deeds.

JM: Faith.

SB: Faith alone is not enough. It's only the beginning. If faith leads to a virtuous life, to a good life, then great. But if it doesn't, it's worthless. Deathbed conversions will take you nowhere, the spirits claim, because you can't fool the universe. You are who you are, and you will gravitate naturally to the proper realm. If you've been a cruel soul you'll gravitate toward a dark region where cruelty is the norm. That's where you will start.

JM: After this first starting phase, then what?

SB: There are ways to progress. It begins by admitting you have fallen short, that you want to be a better person, that you could have done a better job, and that you wish you had. You recognize your deficiency. Then you give yourself, with the instructions of your spirit guide, to service. There are many ways to serve in the spirit world and evolve in the process. You remember your mother-in-law? She's a person who is in a dark place right now. You can help her out of her misery. Go down there and try to reason with her. Let her know that she's loved. Let her know that it's possible to move out of where she's stuck.

JM: What is a spirit guide?

SB: A spirit guide is a former human being, probably long deceased, who has evolved enough to give guidance to those who have newly come over. They have a certain wisdom about them, a more advanced love, and a better tolerance for difficult challenges. That's how they become guides. Many references in this literature say that each of us has at least one spirit guardian until we show them that we have no interest in the help they're trying to give. At that point we can be deserted, and that's a calamitous position to find ourselves in. This is what the communicators are telling us. This and so much more. It's a fascinating world.

JM: As you point out you have fifty different descriptors. The literature is extraordinarily rich.

SB: It is. It is amazing to me that most of the books that I have learned from are out of print, most of them published 100 or 50 years ago. Great material. I read them, looking for commonalities. What I write is based on these.

JM: I know that some of this literature you've decided to discount. You don't take it all at face value.

SB: Some of it strikes me as basically borrowed. A good afterlife account is going to leave me feeling surprised. If I'm not surprised it's probably because some hack or some fraud has brought together the information that I and others have done and decided to make a buck out of it. They might say they are a medium channeling a spirit named such-and-such who is describing their world. There are frauds like that in this literature, unfortunately—actually not that many.

JM: I gather you're looking at, in many cases, mediums who've worked extensively with psychical researchers over decades, who are people who have been known to be of high integrity.

SB: Exactly. Many of them have high reputations. Many of them were British aristocrats—women who didn't have much else to do with their time except to work with these scientists.

Some discovered they had an ability to be good mediums, and they delighted in working with these scientists. It gave them something to do, they became very good at it, and they were people of impeccable reputation, as were the scientists who worked with them.

JM: I'd like to ask you briefly before we close our interview about reincarnation.

SB: Yes, it's affirmed by most of the spirit literature.

JM: Although, not all.

SB: True. I think the reason for that is that if you have not believed in it, if you have hated the very notion of it, and you find yourself in a Christian sector, and you want to communicate through a medium, you still don't believe in reincarnation, even though it's all around you. As soon as you move away from that sector and discover what's really out there, you're probably going change your mind. Why reincarnation? Because of these physical bodies that we have—the dense brains that we're sometimes cursed with and our faulty memories—we are challenged. Our environment is not easy. The more we are challenged, the more progress we can make in a short amount of time.

JM: You mean here in a physical body is actually a very good place for spiritual development.

SB: Absolutely. We're in a spiritual gymnasium. We should make the best of our time, and we should remember that the choices we make here have consequences in the next world.

5

Animals and the Afterlife
with
Miranda Alcott

Jeffrey Mishlove: Hello and welcome. I'm Jeffrey Mishlove. We'll be exploring the subject of animals in the afterlife. With me is Miranda Alcott, an intuitive animal communicator who contributed the chapter "Listening to Water" to the anthology called *The Healing Power of Water* edited by Masaru Emoto. Welcome, Miranda.

Miranda Alcott: Thank you, Jeffrey. It's lovely to be here.

Jeffrey Mishlove: It's a pleasure to be with you, once again. I know you have a lot to say about this subject, meaning that you have had many experiences with animals and their human partners during that transition. Many of our readers may be justifiably skeptical when we talk about the afterlife, especially when based on somebody's intuitions. We'll just regard your intuitive impressions as a source of data. People can do with it as they wish.

Miranda Alcott: Exactly. I'm only here to offer different forms of communication to the human and animal partners after the transition. Most people have impressions about their animals after they've transitioned. Some people will hear their animal's toenails on the ground. Other people will feel the animal jump onto the bed. They want to know, "What does it mean?" and "Is that animal really with me?" those are the basic kinds of questions. Then it goes into a deeper place—which is my favorite place to work—I call it The Intersection, where those two beings still have more to learn from each other.

JM: In other words, the relationship can continue.

MA: Absolutely.

JM: Just as it might with a human.

MA: Yes. Absolutely. When I was very young, I worked with humans who had transitioned but I stopped doing it because I got tired of the client asking questions like, "Where did Aunt Harriet bury the treasure?" That's not the type of work that I prefer to do. The type of work that I am blessed to do is what we still have to learn from each other after one has transitioned. When I counsel people about their animal that has died, it may have been hit by a car and the human is very upset because the animal left its body, or the animal has been sick for a very long time and the animal needs to transition. Other times the human may ask, "My animal is very sick, and I want to know if he's ready to transition. Does he need help, or does he want to be left alone?"

JM: Well, there are many issues that you're raising here. There's the transition process, the grieving process, and the whole metaphysical question about the afterlife itself.

MA: I don't see it as separate but as a continuum because many times after the animal has transitioned, the human is still learning from them. There are still wonderful lessons to be learned and shared. I feel like a very fortunate person, simply because I get to support people through healing, learning and growing along with their animals. As far as I'm concerned, they are all people to me.

JM: Well, you serve as a medium of communication between a deceased animal and a human.

MA: Right, but there are also times when a human has committed suicide and their animal has witnessed it, which is the reverse situation and happens more times than we might hope, obviously. The animal is emotionally shattered because they witnessed the suicide, and they'd tried to help their human feel better. The animal tried to express love in such a way that their human wouldn't feel the need to end their life but, as it turns out, we can't control each other. All they can do is offer, and hopefully provide some recourse after the fact. We can connect with the human and see if there's more learning, healing and growing to be done.

I wanted to mention that sometimes there seems to be a change that happens in whomever has transitioned, whether it's human or animal, where that being seems to have softened. For instance, if the animal in life was cantankerous, jealous or very territorial, the human may expect the discarnate animal to behave the same way it did before it passed out of physical form. But I haven't found that to be true. I have found that the human knows that they're connecting with their friend, because there are tears. They know when they hear something that resonates with them; that it is their animal.

JM: How does your intuition work in this regard? If you're trying to tune in to a deceased animal, how do you find that particular animal and recognize it yourself?

MA: What a great question. I ask if they have a picture or, I'll ask them to describe the animal. I use the animal's energetic patterns to trace the energy to wherever the intersection is, but I don't go in search of it. But I will know if the energy that comes into a gathering shows itself in some form so that we have that exact intersection.

JM: You're not a trance medium.

MA: No.

JM: You're operating, I'm going to say, at a telepathic level, a conscious level and you're picking up impressions and communicating.

MA: Yes. That's right. I'm working from purely an energetic standpoint. If the energy patterning matches, the person will let me know when they identify what they're hearing me say about their animal is accurate.

JM: So, I presume if a human were to transition, you would be able to pick up on them as well.

MA: Yes. The work that I get to do is focused on healing and involvement. We all have lessons we're working on while we're alive but don't usually complete everything in one lifetime. So do the animals. If their spirit happens to be in an animal body, then that's what they are learning about at that time. I connect the animal and the human to the exact intersection where they can still learn from each other and it's very exciting.

JM: You could do that with two humans also, couldn't you?

MA: Yes. And that has happened because I do work with people who've taken their lives and their animals might have witnessed it.

JM: Though I'm not an animal person, I do like them, but I don't have any in my life. That being the case, I have observed that when a pet or animal companion dies, people experience as much grief as if it were a family member.

MA: Or possibly more so. I can't tell you how many people say to me, "This is harder than when I lost my mother," or, "This is harder than when I lost my brother," which is not to berate or lessen those relationships. It's that they had offered their animal companion unconditional love for so long, that it was a part of their everyday lives. So in their perception to not have that relationship any longer can be very challenging.

One thing the animals taught me many years ago is that they aren't actually gone. They would ask me, "Why is it when we leave our bodies that the humans disconnect from us, why do they say because they can't see us, we're not here?" It's an interesting, challenging position to be in, to explain that to someone. Usually, by the time I get the human relaxed, then they are willing to receive that information that comes through for them.

JM: Let's talk a little also about the afterlife itself. I have a hard time conceptualizing it because it seems as if it's a place, like it has a location somewhere.

MA: You know, it's interesting: it depends on the person's belief. Everyone wants to know that their horse has endless amounts of the food that they love. With many dogs, people want to see that they're running on grass and playing with every kind of ball they could want. It depends on the human's belief system that they are holding. I have not found it to be a place but an energetic frequency. It isn't up to me. My job is to provide whatever those two need and to let the human know that their animal has not disappeared. That's another thing that animals say to me, "Please tell my human, stop referring to me in the past. If I were in the past, how could we communicate?" And the human will say, "You mean I can still communicate?" I say yes. Communication works especially well just before you fall asleep. If the client says, "I'm only open to that which is for my highest good," and to allow their animal to come through and telling the animal, "I'm willing to travel with you for a few minutes before I go to sleep." The client is now programmed to go on this journey themselves without needing me.

JM: The spiritualist literature, which I've delved into a bit, suggests that at least in the early stages of being in the afterlife state, we populate it with our own thought forms.

MA: Yes. Absolutely.

JM: And eventually, we may evolve beyond the need to do that and enter a different realm entirely, but there's at least a transitory period where we experience the world around us as we think it should be.

MA: Yes. Exactly. One of the things that I enjoy helping with is when an animal is about to transition through euthanasia. When children are involved, the parents are usually panicking, "Oh my gosh, what do we do with the kids?" One of my favorite things is to suggest that the children draw pictures or write letters to send with the animal so that they can take them on their journey. In fact, those children grow up to be adults who believe that their letters went with their companion, or they can better visualize this step of getting to an afterlife. Children are much more open about this.

JM: I also gather from the afterlife literature, which is vast, that communication doesn't last forever. Sooner or later, the discarnate is going to move into a realm where communicating with the earthly plane is just no longer important.

MA: Right. Either they have new assignments that they receive, or they go back into a purely energetic state. They can go anywhere, and they don't necessarily stay in a conformation of being an animal, a human or with their earthly personality but very much of that soul continues on. That's been my experience, that there is only a certain amount of time.

JM: A window.

MA: Yeah, there's a window, but it can be open for a very long time for some people.

JM: It could be for years.

MA: It can be. When those two beings have more to do together, there are many opportunities for people to teach others without realizing it. For instance, when they talk to a coworker, and the animal's spirit is right alongside them, they say, "I was getting a coffee this morning and I could hear his toenails on the floor and, when I turned around, of course he wasn't there, but I could still hear him." They're teaching when they share that experience along with their animals which are with them for a while. There are many animals who express incredibly articulate guidance to their humans from the afterlife about what they need to work on in their lives: something the human could not hear before. I've worked with people whose animals tried to tell them important things before they left, and the human didn't comprehend it. Once the animal has passed, the human wants to hear what their animal has to say because now they're much more vulnerable and willing to listen. They're willing to be open. They're willing to give it a chance.

JM: What we're touching on now is a topic from a previous interview about things that animals have to teach us. And that's extensive. What you're saying is it goes on even after the transition: that they can be teachers from the other side. Another point you raised in an earlier interview, maybe we can come back to, is the idea of spirit guides and animals.

MA: Animals can become someone's spirit guide, but animals have their own teachers. I don't know that I would call them spirit guides. The human can call them angels, spirit guides, master teachers. Everyone has their own nomenclature.

JM: A Jungian might call them an archetype.

MA: There we are. I haven't found it to be just one way. It's very multiverse.

JM: Would you say that animals and their humans can be together in an afterlife?

MA: In the beginning of the transition many people picture that. I know many people, when their animal has transitioned, want to believe that a relative welcomed their animal. It can happen. As a matter of fact, there are teams that meet up on the other side, which is kind of fun to witness.

JM: Explain that.

MA: For instance, there was a family I worked with that had a couple of animals that transitioned. Suddenly, the wife became very ill and she knew she was going to transition. She wanted to know if anyone was going to be waiting for her. In fact, the dogs were waiting for her with a catcher's mitt. She felt so relieved that it was a wonderful and easy transition, knowing that she was going on to something. I think that hope is a great factor.

JM: You were there. And she's talking to you as it happens?

MA: Oh no. She was with her family, they told me that she saw the animals as she was transitioning. She said, "They're here. Skippy is here," and, "Ah, look at Goo; Goo is here too." She was so excited and lit up.

JM: But if you were there in this circumstance, you might see what she's also seeing.

MA: Yes, as a matter of fact, I've seen what they've seen during transition with humans as well. There was one gentleman who, as he was transitioning, he sat up as he was seeing things. I asked what it was, and he said that I couldn't understand. I asked to see what he was seeing and it looked like a black and white Fellini movie to me. I said to this gentleman, "It's like a Fellini movie." And he said, "How did you know?" As it turned out, he was a film buff, and that surprised me.

JM: I could imagine the afterlife as a Fellini film. As a matter of fact I could get into that.

MA: There you go. Well then, Jeffrey, we'll make sure.

JM: Well, now what about wild animals?

MA: About wild animals?

JM: Do they also have an afterlife? Have you had any experience of that?

MA: I have. I've seen wild animals come back around and hold for their packs or their groups, which is a fascinating experience. There are certain species that will kill their own kind if they become infirm. Animals that are sick are lowering the energy of the rest of the pack. That's fascinating as, after that being transitions, their energy is put back into the pack and they watch over it as well. So, the pack leaders of the animal kingdom will use one of these wise animals, as we might say, as a north star. That relationship goes on for a while until the wise animal moves on either into a pure energetic body or dissipates.

JM: I would assume that reincarnation of animals is also something you might experience.

MA: Yes. I get a lot of questions about that. There are some clients that want their animals to return to them. Then there are people that come and say, "You're not gonna believe this, but I swear this is an animal I had when I was growing up." They do ask whether it is or not. Sometimes it is and sometimes it's another animal that their animal has sent to take care of that human.

JM: I know there's a popular film called "A Dog's Purpose" about a dog that incarnates five or six successive times. So, it's a theme picked up by Hollywood.

That's what you're saying in your authentic, intuitive experience. I call it authentic based on a concept developed by the great psychologist and philosopher William James called radical empiricism. The most direct observations of the world that we get come from our intuitions and observations of our own consciousness. That's real data, just as much to me as if you were reading the dials on a scientific instrument.

MA: I appreciate your sharing that, because for me it has always been real, and it was an adjustment coming into this life. I couldn't believe people didn't know where they had just been and that they didn't hold conversations with the animals in their lives. Why would you draw a line? Those that are alive as humans that are most challenged about being on the planet, are very sensitive beings who have not shut down the right side of their brains. This is a very challenging time to be that sensitive here.

JM: Many of those people are called empaths, for example. And I know they are challenged because we are in a culture that doesn't support it. Our culture is off balance.

MA: It is off balance. Thank you for saying that. I have encouraged many students that have come into my classes who haven't been given credit for being empathic. They're ashamed of it or they're embarrassed about it and it's taken me years to figure out how to deal with it. I entered life excited about all there was and then had to hide it because other people weren't. I was so used to hearing people say, "Well, you're just so sensitive." In fact, my mother would even say, "Well, honey, you're so unique." It was hard to be on the receiving end of these comments, because where I came from, it was a good thing to be sensitive. But in this lifetime, it's something bad. The story I share with my students is that I was having some dental work done and the dentist was complaining about how much Novocaine she had to give me. She said, "Miranda, you are just so sensitive." And I said, "Yes, and that's how I make my living."

JM: Well, indeed you do. The truth is, as you've explained to me in the past, your parents are probably much more supportive than most. They were board members of the American Society for Psychical Research so they were knowledgeable about your sensitivity.

MA: They were, but even they said, "That's fine, honey, just keep it in the house."

JM: Which is sometimes good advice.

MA: Yes, it is, especially when you're growing up because you don't know that other people can't see discarnates or that they can't see other forms of energy.

JM: Well, one of the purposes of this book is to offer a certain amount of validation for people who might be the way you were as a child.

MA: And I appreciate the work that you do, Jeffrey, because you expose all of us to things that we would not otherwise have been exposed to. And it is so important for people to know it's okay to be who they are and to prize their sensitivities instead of trying to hide them.

JM: Well, you know, it takes a certain amount of courage on your part to be interviewed about animals and the afterlife.

MA: I'm excited about it. It's time.

JM: I can tell from the way you're speaking; you don't have any doubt about your perceptions.

MA: No.

JM: You're not questioning this reality at all, are you?

MA: No. You know, I do have limitations but those aren't some of them. We all come in with things to work on.

JM: But doubting yourself isn't one.

MA: Not in this area. I have had too many accurate impressions working with people that transitioned or victims of violent crime, and certainly with my experience on Ground Zero.

JM: You've done a lot of rescue work.

MA: You have to prepare for rescue work on so many levels, especially as a sensitive. So yeah. I've had a lot of experience, I'm happy to say. I've had to determine how to deal with a crisis. How do you do that, being empathic, and not get involved in that energetic?

JM: That's tough. Because, speaking for myself, it's easier to close down than to have to feel other people's pain.

MA: There's something very primal when a person is scream-crying, it resonates inside of us on a vibrational level, fear to the core. It is something that we have to train for, be cognizant of, and have to monitor.

JM: Well, Miranda Alcott, I know we've just scratched the surface of a vast topic. We could talk forever.

MA: Which I would enjoy, because I enjoy listening to you and speaking with you.

6

Spirit Mediumship in Brazil
with
Alexander Moreira-Almeida

~

Jeffrey Mishlove (JM): Hello and welcome. I'm Jeffrey Mishlove. Today we are going to look at the investigation of spirit mediumship in Brazil. Brazil is probably the foremost country in the world where mediumship practices exist and have taken root. My guest is Dr. Alexander Moreira-Almeida, a psychiatrist, a professor of psychiatry. He is editor of several anthologies including *Exploring Frontiers of the Mind-Brain Relationship* and *Spirituality and Mental Health Across Cultures*. Alexander is based in Brazil. Now I'll switch over to the internet video. Welcome Alexander, what a pleasure it is to be with you today.

Alexander Moreira-Almeida (AMA): Thank you very much, Jeff. It's a great pleasure being here. Congratulations for the work you have here at *New Thinking Allowed*.

JM: You've been exploring mediumship and spiritism in Brazil for many years from the perspective of a professional in the field of psychiatry. There are so many different ways to look at it. But I know as a psychiatrist one of the major concerns expressed in the literature has been that people who show mediumistic characteristics are experiencing some form of mental illness.

AMA: Yes, exactly, especially in the mid 19th century in Europe, the United States and even Brazil there was a general understanding usually among the psychologists and psychiatrists that mediumistic experiences and other trance experiences would be a cause or a symptom of mental disorders. We have done studies, not only historical studies from that period, but more recently we are interested in performing psychiatric examinations of mediums to try to see the similarities and differences between mediumistic experience and, for example, psychotic or dissociative disorders.

JM: As I understand it from your research you've come up with a number of examples of individuals who experience symptoms that might otherwise be labeled as psychotic but they've lived healthy, productive, normal lives for decades. As I recall, one of your subjects was in his 90s and had been experiencing these symptoms his entire life without showing any real sign of pathology.

AMA: Exactly, that's the point. Until a few decades ago most studies about psychotic symptoms—for example, hallucination, seeing things, hearing things—most of the studies were performed basically with psychiatric inpatients. The problem is that usually the researchers extrapolated this data from psychiatric inpatients to the general population. But nowadays there have been more and more studies on the general population investigating the prevalence of psychotic experience in the general population. It has been shown that about 15 percent of the people worldwide have reported at least one of these psychotic experiences in the last year. So many studies have been investigating this.

We recently published some papers with in-depth case studies. The one that you are reporting is about Divaldo Pereira Franco. He is the most famous living medium in Brazil. He is now 93 years old. He started having mediumistic experiences—seeing dead people, some precognitive experiences and things like that—when he was four years old. In the beginning he struggled a lot with that. His family did not accept the experience well. He was afraid of being crazy or possessed by the devil. After some time, especially when he was a late teenager, he had contact with spiritism in Brazil and he was received by a spiritist center. He then reframed his experience as mediumistic experience. Since then he has led a very productive life. For example, he has written through mediumistic writing more than 200 books. He has worked regularly as a public servant. He delivers lectures all over the world with no sign of psychotic disorder and things like that.

One of the major points nowadays even in conventional psychiatry has been recognizing that what we call the positive symptoms of psychosis—sensory perception alterations like seeing or hearing things, for example—is not a good marker of pathology of mental disorder. In psychosis, much more indicative of psychotic disorder is cognitive disorganization, impairment in the functioning, or blunted effect and other symptoms like that.

JM: Are you suggesting that this particular individual didn't show those symptoms?

AMA: Exactly. We usually say that in psychosis we have basically three clusters of symptoms. One is more of unusual experiences or positive psychotic symptoms. That usually means perceptual changes, seeing things, hearing things, out-of-body experiences, telepathy and things like that. This is one sort of experience. The second sort of experience we call negative symptoms. For example, people who have difficulties in relationships, in expressing their feelings, people who have less initiative to do things. Also we have the cognitive disorganization symptoms, people who have trouble in reasoning, in paying attention to things and being organized in their lives. Basically, these spiritual non-pathological experiences have more of these unusual experiences, the sensorial experiences and things like that. But they don't have the cognitive disorganization symptoms, the negative symptoms, the loss of motivation and things like that. Specifically in this case, Divaldo Franco, he had a lot of unusual experiences but he didn't have these other types of pathological symptoms.

JM: You mentioned though that in his youth he thought he might be persecuted by devils. You would not consider that necessarily a symptom of cognitive disorganization?

AMA: No, because it fits the cultural background of the person. Before this study we had investigated 115 active mediums in Brazil, in São Paulo. What we found is that most of them did not grow up in a spiritualist family. They usually grew up in a Catholic family or even a Protestant family. But they started having their experiences usually in childhood or adolescence. Their experience was not well accepted by the social environment. These were the two biggest worries that they had: that they were losing their minds, they were becoming crazy, or that they were under demonic influence. This is another very important aspect because usually these non-pathological experiences do not cause suffering or impairment by the experience by itself. However, the impairment or suffering can come from the lack of social support or the cognitive framework that frames this experience in a very negative way: for example, it's a mental disorder or it's a diabolic influence or things like that.

JM: You used the word "reframing" earlier and I think that's very important. It seems as if for people who are having, let's call them paranormal experiences of a subjective nature, in the context of traditional religions that could be viewed as mental illness or diabolic possession. But in the context of spiritism, especially the various spiritistic sects in Brazil and I know there are many, it can be viewed in an entirely different light.

AMA: Yes, exactly, that's the point. There has been a growing recognition that the cognitive framework for this non-pathological experience—paranormal, spiritual or anomalous experience as a whole—it's very important to determine if it will have a positive or negative influence on these people. But it's also very important to keep in mind that I do not deny at all the existence of psychotic disorders, the existence of schizophrenia or other disorders. At the same time, we have several people having non-pathological anomalous experiences labeled as people having mental disorders. We also can have it the other way around: people having truly psychotic disorders that are in need of antipsychotic medication and the patients themselves, but also relatives, even religious leaders; they deny that it is a mental disorder and they claim that's just a spiritual experience or things like that. Because of that there is a huge delay in starting treatments with severe impact in the prognosis of these patients.

JM: I'm under the impression that maybe more than any other country, Brazil has a culture that favors the practice of mediumship in many different contexts. Would you say that's true?

AMA: I can say that in Brazil mediumship is something usually well accepted in the country, despite most Brazilians being Catholics. We also have a large number of Protestants. But the third largest religion group is Spiritism and the fourth largest religion group are African-Brazilian religions. These last two have a strong emphasis on mediumistic experience. But even among Catholics in Brazil many of them are very open to mediumistic experiences. It's quite frequent in Brazil for a person to be a Catholic but at the same time attend spiritist centers, watch lectures, receive some treatments, read spiritualist books and things like that. Just to give an example, there is a national survey in Brazil showing that half of Catholics in Brazil believe in reincarnation. This is a very widespread belief in Brazil.

JM: Spiritism in Brazil really goes back to Allan Kardec in France; that's his pen name. You have written a fascinating paper. Many people today think of Kardec as the founder of a religion but you point out that he approached this phenomenon as an academic expert in pedagogy, or the science of education, and that his approach was largely quite skeptical, at least initially.

AMA: Yes, exactly. Allan Kardec was a French scholar from the mid 19th century. He was a member of several scientific societies in France in that period. He was much in favor of free thinking and things like that. He started investigating mediumistic experiences because there was a huge interest in western Europe and the United States in the mid 19th century: the modern spiritualism. So he started to investigate this. He took at first a more skeptical approach. He thought it could be some physical force or unconscious activity or a fraud. But later, after his studies, he became convinced that of course it could be fraud, it could be unconscious mind activity, it could be telepathy, but also in many cases they were caused by deceased spirits through mediumship. So Kardec himself created the word spiritism when he published *The Book of Spirits* in 1857. In this book he created the word spiritism, spiritist, and things like that. He claimed that spiritism was not a religion but it was a spiritualist philosophy that was developed based on his scientific investigations. But he also stressed that this philosophy had strong ethical, or perhaps spiritual, implications but not organized as a religion with dogmas and things like that.

JM: I understand that his methodology was one we might call today one of consensus: that he would interview different mediums in trance. When seven different mediums—I think that's the number he selected—were all in agreement on some particular point he would consider that a form of authentication.

AMA: He compared mediums with microscopes or telescopes. They would be instruments that would allow us to see the unseen. That would be the idea. And, yes, he tried to use as many mediums as he could. Actually, he developed an impressive network in more than forty different countries around the globe connected with hundreds of people in different continents having contact with mediums and things like that. He developed a huge network and he had made contacts with these researchers and people who work with mediums in different countries. He himself investigated many different mediums in France and Switzerland, for example. He tried as much as he could to have similar questions or to investigate some phenomena in different mediums to see if there are similarities. For example, what these alleged deceased spirits would claim how they behave; what were the consequences of their actions in the previous life, and things like that. Based on this investigation and putting together and checking different information from different mediums he developed spiritism.

JM: In your work I think one of the most important questions that you've looked at is whether or not mediums in trance are able to access forms of information through paranormal means that turn out to be valid.

AMA: Yes. Our first way to investigate mediums was first to check the mental health of those mediums. Is this just a mental disorder or a symptom of a mental disorder or not? So after years of investigating different ways it was clear that mediums usually are mentally sane, mentally healthy. If they are not psychotic, what are these experiences? This is the next major question. Based on that, we have performed investigations in neuroimaging studies, trying to investigate how the brain works. Another way to investigate what is the ultimate nature of this experience: we try to investigate if mediums can produce information about a deceased person; for example, information that they could not possibly have by natural means, through contact with the relatives of the deceased or in the press or whatever. We have developed different strategies to perform this research to investigate if mediums actually have access to what we call anomalous information reception.

JM: Anomalous information reception. That's a lovely term. I know in particular you focused on one of the most famous mediums of the 20th century, Chico Xavier.

AMA: Yes. Our first study on this topic about anomalous information reception among mediums was with Chico Xavier. Chico Xavier was the most prolific medium in Brazil. He died in 2002. He wrote more than 400 books through mediumistic writing: what they called psychography, a kind of automatic writing. He donated all copyrights to charity. He never received any money payments or donations to himself because of his mediumistic work. He retired as a low-level public servant and all his life he lived a very humble life. He died at almost 90 years old having a very humble life. One of the most interesting aspects of his mediumship [is that] the first part of his mediumship was strongly devoted to writing books. But the last decades of his life were devoted more to writing letters to those who lost their loved ones. These letters were allegedly written by the deceased.

For example, a young man who died in a car crash wrote a letter to his parents. We investigated some of these letters. The limitation of this study is that it was a retrospective study so we were not present when the letters were written. But we were able to get the letters; we were able to interview the relatives and other people that were related to that to investigate what kind of information was passed to Chico Xavier and what kind of information was in the letters and what were the possibilities of Chico Xavier having access to these pieces of information. What we found in the studies that we published—we published some papers on this topic—was that these letters had a high level of precise information and [with] most of them we could not trace a way in which Chico Xavier could have access to this information. There were several very specific [pieces of] information, for example, about the childhood of the deceased person, about very private matters in the family that only the father knew: experiences that he himself had that no one else in the family knew about. This information was in the letters.

JM: I understand that when you say highly accurate we're talking about well over 90 percent accuracy.

AMA: Yes. [There was much] specific information, as I said, about the way of dying, the way of living, names of relatives, deceased and living relatives, names of places. Really, very specific information, most of [which], to our knowledge, was not passed to the medium.

JM: This is not just a single letter. This is a level of accuracy that you and your colleagues observed over numerous letters of this sort developed through the mediumship of Chico Xavier.

AMA: Chico Xavier wrote probably thousands of these letters, but we published the studies of two sets of letters that relate to two different deceased people. In one paper we analyzed only one letter and in the other paper we analyzed 13 letters related to another specific deceased person. It will be very important if we could have more studies on this topic. But because of this limitation, because it's a retrospective study we cannot know for sure what kind of information was passed to the medium. We started to develop new prospective studies. We have developed and published some new studies with living mediums. In those studies we were able to control what kind of information was passed to the mediums.

JM: Did the same level of accuracy show up in the prospective studies?

AMA: In the first study we basically replicated the triple blind design of mediumistic studies that were developed in the United States and the UK. In Brazil what usually happens, [is that] the medium is in a spiritual center or someplace like that. Usually there is a meeting once a week, once a month, or something like that where people who lost their loved ones recently go there and try to have contact or receive a letter. That's the point. Usually we have dozens or hundreds of people in the same meeting asking for this sort of information. Usually they have a small contact with the medium: a very brief interview, a few seconds or a few minutes. The mediums claim that it's useful to make a connection, to see if they will be able to be in contact with the deceased.

In the first study we developed this triple blind protocol but the most experienced mediums in writing these kind of letters did not accept to take part in the study. They said that it was too different, too artificial for them to perform this sort of study where they could have no contact at all with the sitters, with their relatives, and any other sorts of controls that they thought was very unnatural to them. So they did not accept. But we were able to recruit other mediums, other experienced mediums but not that experienced in writing these sort of letters. In this first study we had negative results. We were not able to show that mediums produced information above chance because in the end the sitters received their letters, the letter intended for them, and five other control letters, but they did not know which letter was for them. They had to choose one of the letters but they were not able to choose the right one above chance. We were not able to show any sort of anomalous information reception in this study.

It raised among us the question about what we call ecological validity. If the method was appropriate to that subject of study, the mediums. We developed a different protocol. We interviewed very experienced mediums in producing these kinds of letters and tried to figure out what would be the environment that they would feel comfortable working in. At the same time, we tried to include all sorts of controls for any kind of information that would be passed from the relatives to the medium. This is exactly the kind of study that we perform. So what happened? We selected the sitters, the ones who were grieving for a loved one in the last two years. We selected these people and we selected the mediums, but they did not know each other previously. The mediums were far from our city because we developed this research here in Juiz de Fora in the Minas Gerais state in Brazil. The relatives were from this region but the mediums were from at least 400 miles away from here. So the sitters and the mediums, they never had previous contact. [During] the only contact that they had, we were video recording everything. We were able to see every word, everything that the relative could have told or exhibited to the medium. Usually they had very short contact: usually a few seconds or at most two minutes; a very brief conversation. After that the medium wrote the letters.

Based on that we are now investigating if the letters contain information that could not be inferred from the information that they got in the séance. We just published the first paper now, describing the protocol as a whole. In this study we involved three mediums, 142 sitters and we had 26 letters. The mediums and the sitters felt very comfortable with the protocol. It was also interesting that the level of belief in paranormal experience, the level of spirituality, did not predict who would receive the letter. As I said, we had 142 sitters but only 21 of them received letters. We tried to see what would be the predictor of receiving a letter. The only predictor was the severity of grief. The severity of grief predicted the likelihood of receiving the letter. At the end of this study 96 percent of the sitters considered the letters to be definitely or probably from the deceased relative. We are now analyzing in detail each letter to investigate if they have or do not have anomalous information that could not be explained in regular ways. We hope some of these papers will be published very soon.

JM: I wonder if mediumship isn't in some ways parallel to remote viewing, which is a popular practice here in the United States where you have some star performers who can routinely come up with accuracy close to a hundred percent and then you have hundreds of other people entering the field whose accuracy is sometimes very good but oftentimes they experience what they call displacement or they're simply not accurate for reasons that we don't yet understand.

AMA: Actually, I think any sort of paranormal experience or spiritual experience is similar to any other human skill. For example, in Brazil we love soccer. We can have a big soccer star. In a certain game he performs splendidly. In the next game he performs awfully. So the same person with the same team performs very differently because there are so many variables that can influence the performance. But it happens in any skill. For example, I'm also a professor at the university. Sometimes I deliver the same lecture, and one day I think, "Oh, it was splendid." The other day, that lecture was not good. But I am the same person delivering the same content but the environment, my state of spirit, everything changed. I think it's exactly the same with any other human skill. If it's not like that it can perhaps even raise suspicions about that skill specifically.

So definitely, I agree with you. I think there are some mediums that can perform more consistently at a much higher level, but even those also had their bad days. Leonora Piper, one of the most famous and most studied mediums, a Bostonian woman from the 19th century, was an example. On the good days she produced a high level of very precise information: a large amount of it. On other days, she produced inaccurate information and things like that. So I think with mediums the point is how can we stimulate or create the environment to allow mediums to perform in a better way, but at the same time that we could control and analyze in a proper way to avoid fraud and other conventional explanations.

JM: I would imagine that your position as a professor of psychiatry puts you in a sort of unique perspective looking at this, especially since in some sense the spiritist community is in competition with the psychiatric community, in that many social services and mental health cases are handled through the spiritist centers.

AMA: Actually, I don't think there is a competition. More and more we think that there is a complementary approach, specifically in the academic environment. We work in spirituality as a whole. Until last year I was the chair of the section on spirituality of the World Psychiatric Association. The point is not to impose any religious or spiritual beliefs and not to replace psychological or psychiatric treatment to patients. The point is to develop a real bio-psycho-social-spiritual approach to people, taking into consideration the biological, psychological, social and spiritual aspects. Definitely, I think we need to move on, to go beyond this idea of competition that unfortunately was very prevalent in last century and even in the current century. Religious groups in opposition to medical groups or medical groups in opposition to psychology, and psychology with psychiatry. Of course, we don't need this to value spirituality. We don't need to deny the biology or the psychology or whatever. I think that is the major point.

But coming back to your question about spiritism and providing support. Yes, in Brazil we have a very specific and interesting experience: the spiritist-psychiatric hospitals. Dozens of these hospitals were founded in Brazil in the last century. These spiritist-psychiatric hospitals were not only spiritists: they had psychiatrists—they still do; they are still working. They have psychologists, psychiatrists, social workers, nurses, and also spiritual support for the patients. Also, in spiritist centers it is very common for people seeking help for spiritual healings and other practices like that. Spiritist centers usually recommend people to go to their doctors, to the psychologists and so on, but also to seek spiritual support. I think that we can learn more and more how to work in a collaborative work because our goal must be the well-being of the population.

JM: In other words, it would seem as if in Brazil there's more cooperation between the medical community, particularly the psychiatric community, and the spiritist community than one would find in other countries. In the United States I think such cooperation is pretty much negligible.

AMA: Yes, but it's not so easy. Many psychiatrists and psychologists are very suspicious about anything about religion, about spirituality. Psychiatry and psychology in Brazil have a strong influence from European and North American schools. For example, psychoanalysis from Freud. Freud had a strong influence in Brazil and still has, especially nowadays in psychology, and he usually had very negative views of spirituality, of religion. Sometimes they are very suspicious about that. But many other professionals are quite open to this. Actually, there are some current studies about the spirituality of psychologists and psychiatrists in Brazil showing that, by and large, most of them are spiritual and religious persons and they are open to taking into consideration the spirituality of patients. In Brazil we also have a non-academic organization, the Medical Spiritist Association, that congregates people who are spiritists and physicians to discuss the implications between spiritism and health.

JM: Brazil is also unique in the sense that some of the great mediums like Chico Xavier have been publicly honored by the country as a whole. For example, I believe, many years ago Chico Xavier himself appeared on Brazilian postage stamps.

AMA: Yes. Chico Xavier, specifically because of his charitable enterprise, he has always been so humble in helping people and also developing social assistance to many people in need. He received a lot of respect in Brazil. I think about 20 years ago there was a survey in Brazil where people could vote for the Brazilian of the century. He was among the most voted for the Brazilian of the century. We also had some movies, some very good movies about Chico Xavier and another about the life of Divaldo Franco. These two movies were very popular. Chico Xavier books sold dozens of millions of copies until now. So definitely, it's very popular; it's very respected, usually because of their examples of life.

JM: You mentioned that he lived a humble life. He worked as a low-level public servant throughout his life even while he was writing hundreds of books through some form of spiritual dictation called psychography. I'm under the impression that by donating the royalties from all of these books to charity, we're talking about tens of millions of dollars he donated to help poor people.

AMA: Exactly. In spiritism, as Allan Kardec emphasized, mediums should not be paid by mediumship. They believe that mediumship is a gift from God that people received for free and should give for free. Since Allan Kardec, in spiritism there is a strong emphasis in mediumship as a charitable practice and that people should never ever receive any personal benefits from this. Because of this, in all spiritist centers in Brazil, the mediumship is always for free; you never have to pay anything. Chico Xavier and Divaldo Franco are two examples of that.

JM: Have you done any studies comparing the Afro-Brazilian styles of mediumship with the spiritist approach?

AMA: We published a study a few years ago with Umbanda. Umbanda is the most common African-Brazilian religion. A female Umbanda priest is called *mãe-de-santo*. It was an in-depth study of a prominent Umbanda priest in Brazil. The story is very similar to Divaldo Franco's. She started in childhood having precognitive dreams. She started having spontaneous trance possession. She was also not well accepted by her relatives, her parents, and so she struggled with that. She tried to suppress this experience. She tried to avoid and not tell anyone about this. It caused a lot of struggles. But after some time, I don't remember exactly, but about in her mid-twenties she went to an African-Brazilian center, an Umbanda center, and there she started to understand in a new light; she reframed her experience and received support. In the next years she became a prominent Umbanda leader, an Umbanda priest in Brazil. This is the only study that we have performed with African-Brazilian religions. But definitely it is important to have more studies on this topic also.

JM: Alexander, it's been a real pleasure exploring this fascinating world that you live in. From our perspective here in North America you're in a very exotic country and yet you're approaching it with all the tools of modern western science and all of the cultural resources there in Brazil. You're in a very unique position. I'm looking forward to future interviews with you exploring the details of your research even further. Alexander, thank you so much for being with me today.

AMA: Jeff, thank you for the opportunity to talk to you and to talk to your audience to discuss what I always call human experiences. We need to know, to understand the human experience as a whole. What are we as human beings? This experience that we have here in Brazil is not only here in Brazil. Perhaps in Brazil people are more open to this kind of experience. But definitely this is a kind of experience that happens in any country, in any place and throughout history. I think it is very important to respect these experiences but at the same time using the tools of science that we have to try to have a better understanding about the grasping of this experience. Thank you very much for this opportunity.

JM: For those of you watching or listening, thank you for being with us.

7

The Afterlife and the Unconscious Mind
with
Betty Kovács

Jeffrey Mishlove: Today we'll be exploring the afterlife and the unconscious mind. My guest is Dr. Betty Kovács who has taught symbolic and mythic language for many years. She serves on the advisory board of the Forever Family Foundation. She is the author of *The Miracle of Death: There is Nothing but Life*, as well as *Merchants of Light: The Consciousness That is Changing the World*. We're going to be exploring the afterlife and how it impacts us at the unconscious or the subconscious level of the mind.

In your book, *The Miracle of Death*, you report many communications with your deceased son and your deceased husband that are mediated through something we've discussed earlier, the language of the soul.

Betty Kovács: I prefer the phrasing "the language of soul" or "the organ of soul" even more than "the unconscious" because I think that there's so much more to it than we have comprehended regarding Jung's use of the words unconscious or subconscious.

JM: I'm under the impression that Jung himself believed that the afterlife existed within what he called the collective unconscious.

BK: Yes. It just seems that it exists everywhere. It's almost like it's contained inside the field of fields for it to be accessible everywhere. Perhaps that would be "the organ of soul" through which it can operate within the human mind.

JM: Of course, William Blake, the great poet, said if we could just see things as they really are we would know that everything is infinite. This concept suggests that we're already living simultaneously in every world. The afterlife is with us constantly.

BK: That's a beautiful way of putting it. I think it's exactly right, that it's always here. It's just like our ancestors thought of the three worlds. The world of pure mind: pure intelligence, that is perpetually coming into being in the subtle world. When it touches that subtle world, it shapes itself into laws. We recognize these laws as archetypes. These are the essential structures of the universe. We are the ones in time and space who are perpetually in touch with the subtle world, if indeed we truly haven't cut ourselves off from it.

What is so important to remember is that these three worlds are always together. They're perpetually coming into being and moving so that everything is infinite.

As Blake said so beautifully, "the universe in a grain of sand." If only we could hold that vision of how everything is perpetually merging into beingness.

JM: Of course, it's hard to go about our daily life with that thought constantly in mind. People have to brush their teeth and take care of their daily chores. "Chop wood and carry water" as the Zen Buddhists would say.

As we become more engrossed in the physical world over the course of our lives, we tend to lose sight of that mystical vision, that sense of the infinite.

BK: I think, though, that there will be a time (or at least that there can be a time) when we will remain aware that we are perpetually one, always moving and coming into being.

We speak today of the left brain, fearing that it gets in the way of the symbolic brain, fearing that the rational mind will interrupt if we want to just try to be present in the dream or the vision.

When we learn how to allow that energy of consciousness, which exists infinitely, to flow through the spinal cord, up through all the brain components (with the right, symbolic brain feeding into the left, rational brain), then as Giambattista Vico imagined, there would be this perpetual continuum of movement between these minds so that even when we brush our teeth we would have that awareness, that presence of being.

JM: It does sound like a beautiful image. I think it's one that I aspire to. I'm a long way from being there. I'm probably further along though than many people, I suspect, because I've been having conversations like this one with people just like you for a long time.

In your book, *The Miracle of Death*, you detailed encounters with István and Pisti, your deceased husband and son. As I read the manuscript again, they seem to be almost entirely at the symbolic level; very rarely are they at the literal level. Or am I wrong about that?

BK: What do you mean by the literal level?

JM: Conversations that might be like the one that we're having right now, sort of back and forth, linear in some way, one word following another.

BK: It really was like a conversation and that's what was so beautiful and convincing about it. Of course, we were experiencing something that was rare and mystifying. This was especially apparent to my husband because he had never been concerned with those kinds of unfathomable matters.

An interesting aside here is that in one vision he asked Pisti, "I wonder why I was never concerned with these things?" and Pisti said because they were of the same soul. They were twin souls.

He said to his dad, "Had you continued as you were as a child with those concerns, you and mom might not have been able to conceive me. So, you had to put yourself on ice until I stepped into the other world."

It was true. After Pisti died, István would come into my study and say, "What should I read next? I've got to make up for 50 years."

As for my own experiences with Pisti, he was very present, although I didn't see him as an image; I felt him as an energy, and I knew where that energy was in the room. My husband and Pisti's girlfriend, Jenny, both saw the image. Pisti told his dad that it wouldn't be good for me to see the image because as a mother I'd always been concerned with the image, keeping it well, where it is.

It was very important to let go of that image so that the energy could be present, but not the image. So, it was very much his presence. I would think one thing and he would answer it.

JM: It's very interesting to me to try and get a handle on this because I cannot say that I've ever had detailed exchanges of this sort with any of my departed loved ones or friends. I have the impression from your description that they are energy beings more than embodied beings.

BK: Oh yes, not embodied. His consciousness was present, extremely present, just fully present in a way. At least it felt fully present based on what I had experienced. It was so healing for us that we did have those experiences with him. It helped us.

It was a fantastically powerful healing experience for us because we realized that he is in another dimension, yet he's here and he is still creating and that's what he wanted us to remember.

It was always like this: he didn't want to tell us something; he wanted us to remember it as if all of us really know all of this; it's just we can't remember it.

It was interesting with István, my husband, because before Pisti died I had been working with shamans from South America and I had an experience in which it was very clear to me in that vision that they were of the same soul.

In fact, I was told, "You thought you actually agreed to name Pisti 'Pisti'." I remember my chair in the English department said, "You're not going to name him that, are you?" The firstborn had been named that for a long time and I finally thought, why not, that's fine. But in the vision, it was said, "You thought that you made that decision, but he could not have been named anything else. They are both of the same soul." When I came home, I didn't tell my son anything about the vision. Except I said, "I had an experience in which it seemed that you and your dad were of the same soul."

He was painting something; he didn't even turn around. He said, "Oh, it sounds about right."

István said the same thing, so I didn't say any more about it. A couple of years later, during István's first vision with Pisti, Pisti told his dad that they were of the same soul. And not only told him, but they also experienced it. So, it wasn't just conversation. István said that he felt like he shot out of his body and was going through a long funnel in which he saw many souls on both sides. He saw faces that were his own face, he saw others that were Pisti's face and then he saw many people in which they were with one face. When there were two people, Pisti would talk to him about that experience. When they were one, István just knew it. These experiences were a combination of knowing and finding out more about ourselves, and also connecting to that spirit world as though that spirit world is right here with us all the time.

JM: I think for clarity of our readers who may not understand the full story we should say that Pisti died first and István died a year or two later?

BK: Two years later. It was a very powerful time in our lives. First, my mother was killed by a car and then one year later our son was in a car accident. He was in the trauma center for 13 days when the doctors decided to take him off life support.

We learned that he wouldn't make it on exactly the day my mother had been killed one year before, on the same date and the same hour. I had nothing to do with it; synchronicities were happening.

It was really during that period after Pisti's death that István and I had many experiences until István was killed. He went to Hungary to visit his family. He also had business there. He left on that trip, and he never came back. He was killed there.

I did have experiences with István afterwards, but we had most of our experiences with our son during that time before István's death.

JM: Also, for clarity, for our readers, I think it's correct to say that the names István and Pisti are both Hungarian.

BK: Yes. István was born in Hungary and fought in the revolution and escaped into Yugoslavia and then came as a refugee to the United States.

JM: In other languages I can understand where somebody might question, "Why are you naming your son Pisti?"

BK: I know! It's a very interesting thing, P-i-s-t-i, and of course, when he went to school the teacher pronounced it "Pistee." When we picked him up one day, he had a name tag on that read "Steve" and that just happened to be the translation.

István said to him, "Well, who's that?" and he said, "It's me." So, he went with all his friends as Steve. When I told him, "Do you realize that's really the translation of your name?" Well, no he didn't. There was a character named Steve and I think that's why he chose the name. He was not going to have his name pronounced that way in school, so he had two names growing up.

JM: You know, with my name Mishlove I also encountered a lot of teasing when I was a child.

BK: I can imagine!

JM: Growing up in the Midwest of the United States my Jewish last name drew some attention.

Back to our topic here, you describe István and Pisti after their demise as being in another dimension. What I'm curious about is the relationship of that other dimension to what we think of as our own consciousness.

BK: I think it's all one. I do think it's all one. I think we differentiate it given our culture and our experience or, more accurately speaking, our lack of experience. I think it is all one; it's perpetually being.

Yet because we live in time and space, we put these things in different realms and different categories. As you said, we do have to brush our teeth and buy the groceries and that sort of thing, and I think then we sort of close a certain part of our awareness off.

As Aldous Huxley has said, there's a valve. We're all born into universal mind; it's always who we are: it's always present. But we have a valve that we have to kind of close and just allow a trickle of it to flow through so that we can do these things in ordinary daily life. Then as we grow accustomed to our lives with age, it's as though we forget how to release that valve.

If we just release the valve, we find that we are where we've always been.

JM: There's a passage from Homer's *Odyssey* where Odysseus goes to the underground temple, and he communicates with his deceased mother. They're having an interaction and then all of a sudden, many other spirits notice that something like a channel of communication is open, and the spirits come flooding through that frequency. They all want to talk through the channel to reach Odysseus. He has to shut it down, otherwise, it would be overwhelming with too many spirits wanting to come through.

BK: Mediums talk about that, about a flood of people coming through and they all want to talk and get their message through.

I'm thinking this is surely a result of our having practically closed off our minds as a species to this other dimension. If all of us were able to release that valve and be present and allow the past, present, and future to be present now, what we call the other world, the underworld, all of it would be present.

If we knew how to do that, we probably wouldn't have that situation of spirits just absolutely knocking themselves over to get through. There must be such an effort to get through to people they love on the other side, to help us to know they're okay, they're creating, they'll see us again.

JM: In previous conversations we talked about different times in human history where people did seem more open to this other world than at other times. I would imagine that maybe in the most ancient times that you write about, the cave cultures, people were the most open to this interpenetration of the dimensions.

BK: Yes, I think certainly from all the evidence, they had the rituals, they set aside the time and they had the place where they could be present. Also, later, during the megalithic period, the structures were utilized to help us keep in touch with the rhythms of the earth and the cosmos.

There's always been that information from the ancestors—that we need to know these laws of nature because they are the laws of our soul, our psyche.

If we can live in harmony with the laws of the cosmos, it will open these dimensions of our own soul. The human being was seen as the mediator between the earth energies and the cosmos. To really do that must be a tremendous feeling and presence in life. I just think we can be so much more present.

I had struggled all my life to know something beyond what I knew. When I first went to South America and they were talking about the visionary state, we'd have these rituals to open the visionary mind. They did work with San Pedro. When the shaman came to me, I said, "Listen, give me double because I never can get in touch with anything. I just get caught in the rational brain."

He almost did, but it just was so hard. Certainly, our ancestors had figured that out. They knew through knowledge of certain sacred plants. There were so many sacred plants that would help [to] open and release that valve.

That's what sacred plants do. They release the valve.

We know that probably happened in the cave cultures because there were sacred plants available in Europe at that time. I think that there was the knowledge in these cultures that we can experience our vastness and then let the valve return to its place so we can operate in everyday life.

There's a beauty to that too: to play the game of matter, of coming in and being individuals and loving each other and seeing their uniqueness and developing the uniqueness. It's a wonderful game to play.

And, of course, we have to experience the deaths of those people. Even if we know the game we're playing, it's still a grief. But we also know the joy of the larger game.

JM: I'm under the impression from earlier interviews I've done with Stephanie Stephens who is a Jungian scholar writing about Carl Jung's interactions with the dead about which he writes quite extensively in his autobiography and in the *Red Book*, Jung seems to feel that there's a distinction between the archetypal images of the unconscious mind and the actual dead.

I would think that for anybody opening themselves up to this area, it would be logical to question: if I'm having such an experience, is it an archetypal projection from my subconscious mind or is this an authentic communication?

BK: That's one thing I didn't worry too much about because if there is pure intelligence moving into the subtle world, it immediately takes the shape of these essential structures, it immediately takes the shape of these laws. I think that these laws are archetypes. I'll try to give an example of the difference.

István would be with Pisti, and they knew each other: they knew what was going on and were talking. In the first vision István realized suddenly that there was a feminine being with them and that she had always been with them. Then he allowed himself to just really experience this being and he said, "She was the most beautiful being I had ever seen, but she had no face."

I couldn't help but think of the prehistoric goddesses with no face. At any rate, he became aware of this. She talked with him, and he realized this presence, this essence of the universe, this feminine loving creative essence.

She even said that her name was Sira. It would be pronounced Sheera in Hungarian.

I thought it was interesting that she even gave him a name. I think I would call that an archetypal being. Just a few weeks before he went to Hungary, when he was killed in the automobile accident there, he told me that she was always in all his visions after that.

In one vision he was at Machu Picchu and there was a waterfall there—I've never seen a waterfall at Machu Picchu—but there was in this vision. István said then he saw Sira or this feminine being in the waterfall. He said she was ancient and then she would become beautiful, a young woman, but she would go between these two opposite appearances.

He then stepped into the waterfall and merged with her.

I think this is an archetypal experience. It wasn't someone who had been in this world and died. She was much vaster than that. I then started experiencing her very profoundly in my visions.

I asked Pisti one time: I said, "Pisti, I'm having trouble understanding this. I feel she's an archetypal being, but she's so personal. She's intimate and cosmic." Then he said, "Mom, she is so vast her body covers solar systems and galaxies."

I thought to myself, did my mind make that up?

I was absolutely stunned many years later when I was reading Mary Rodwell who works with children who seem to know that they are from non-human intelligences, not of the earth. They believe that they have agreed to be born into their human lives to help us through this evolutionary phase. One of those children said, "My memory of where I came from was a body so vast it covered solar systems and galaxies." There was that same descriptive language.

I don't know what to do with that, but I certainly found it interesting. At least I no longer thought, well, I had just made that up. There's something vast about the consciousness that exists in the universe.

Does it appear to us as an archetype? I have some questions about that, but I leave it open.

JM: If I could summarize what I'm getting from this discussion: we started out by talking about the one mind that we all share, and it seems to me this one mind is infinite and it can be divided up infinitely in many different ways so that when we delve into the depths of our own minds we may encounter deceased loved ones; we may encounter devas, deities, archetypes, extraterrestrials, creatures from other planets; the possibilities are pretty much infinite.

BK: I think you've exactly said it, yes, it's infinite possibilities. There's no beginning and no end, it seems. István had a vision of universes coming into being and then dissolving, but he said not necessarily even in that order. It was the most magnificent thing he was allowed to experience. He said, "I had the mind of a physicist. I understood it."

Pisti reminded him, "Dad, when you go back, you won't remember what you do now as a physicist." At any rate, he realized that he was both that universe that was coming into being and going out; he was everything at once; it was everything at once. We were all playing these very different roles in a masterful game.

JM: I have the sense that this experience of *everything at once,* that is the true reality. You and I, here communicating as we do electronically in the modern world; it all seems so very real to our external senses, but at a deeper level this is the illusion that we're separate.

BK: Exactly, in almost all visionary experiences and dreams we realize that we are one. We also learn as creators how to create the uniqueness of each thing, each person one might say.

I don't think we can do that without the uniqueness of everybody else. I think that the wholeness, the unity, is not as simple as we just go back into a coalescent blob. I think we go back as unique beings to the degree that we've been able to create that uniqueness and we take all that knowledge and that novelty to the wholeness, but it's all one.

Getting the glimpse that we're all one is a wonderful thing and then it's also wonderful to come back in and try to play an infinitely variant game, to try to do something that's creative.

Which it is; it is the essence of creativity.

I had one of the most profound experiences before Pisti died: more profound than my work with the shamans from South America. I was at Machu Picchu, and I was up above looking down at my dead body. I saw these spirits just moving my body on a gurney across the mountain. I knew they were taking it to Huayna Picchu, which is thought of as the ancient old woman of the mountain.

I thought, oh great, I'm going to be admitted to the mountain. These spirits, these beings, will give me the secrets of the universe. Well, we got right up to the mountain, and it stopped, no entry, and then, Boom! Suddenly I realized I was the mountain. I was that gurney. I was that dead body. I was those spirits. But, of course, it wasn't in that linear fashion.

Suddenly I had the experience of, "We are it," as Alan Watts used to say.

Then I found myself in a forest realizing I'm a creator and I sat there, and I said, but I can't create a world. The voice that came was so moving to me. It said, "Oh, you just did create a world in which you cannot create. That's the world you created. We can do nothing but create." That was so moving to me to realize all this negative lack of confidence: "I can't do that," that's what I was creating.

JM: In other words, there's some, you might even call it a secret reason that we have decided to embed ourselves in this world as mortal beings with all the limitations that we face.

BK: Yes. There's something in all of this that we can use for some vaster, greater reason.

JM: It strikes me as well that even though I think it is ultimately an illusion or, as the Hindu sometimes say, *maya*, from the point of view of a mortal being, as we both are, it's really quite real, and from this perspective it is important to try and distinguish, let us say, between a psychological projection and an authentic psycho-spiritual communication.

BK: Yes. I've always had trouble with the word illusion, or *maya* as illusion, because I think it's a reality we have created for various purposes. I wonder about the projections. We do need to think of those things and work with them, but there are certain archetypes that we experience, or the dead who make very clear they're very much alive.

I should clarify, the only people who were dead, so to speak, that I talked with were István and Pisti except that twice I did see my mother. It was more in activity or what was happening, but we didn't really speak with each other. I have no ability to speak with others except those two.

For instance, the jackal had come to me and to István. I think that, as the Egyptian gods were archetypes, the jackal is an archetype. He was an archetype of that energy within us that can transform what we call dead or decayed into new life. We all have that ability of the imaginal cells.

I think he is that. But there was one experience with—I don't know whether they were archetypal beings or real beings from other dimensions; I had probably one of the most powerful experiences I've ever had in my life.

I and two other women were doing a ritual for children, for the earth—Pisti hadn't died yet even at that point. I talk about it in both books—but there was a huge disc that I experienced, that came. I saw it; my eyes were closed and it came through the sliding glass doors, and it hovered over my head. I knew that it was the most powerful cosmic consciousness. It was filled with consciousness far too great for me to experience.

Then out of the bottom of it swirled a being. I felt she took form in a limited way so that I could experience them. She went right down through the crown chakra and into my heart. I saw that she had to her waist a white satin dress and she had a white satin square hat. So here we had a mandala with a round disc and a square hat.

I have never in my life experienced that kind of consciousness. She sang through me, "We are here. You have called us, and we have come. Your planet has called us, and we are here. Can you feel us?"

It was just the most incredible feeling of this consciousness. She said to the three of us, "We are here for you all three. We are the light that circles around your planet. She told us, "We are ready to connect to your planet."

I felt this was an archetypal experience that we were having, but that it was also an experience that the species and the earth were having because the light had been there. We had drawn that light to us and now it was powerful enough, this love, light and consciousness on our planet, that we could pull it to the planet and connect it.

That's what she was saying. She said, "You have connected this day to all those people on your planet who are creating worlds of love and peace."

I was so exhausted after that experience. One of the women was kind of a large woman and she somehow intuitively knew— we simply lay on the floor, and she just held me, like holding me together for maybe an hour. I just couldn't move. It was so powerful.

But I could ask if that was archetypal. Or was it non-human intelligences, this huge ship filled with intelligence far too powerful for me to experience unless it did reduce itself, the frequency, so that I could experience it.

When I was still in my doubting period, before the deaths even I would say, I went to Europe right after that, and I would always revisit the moment with the notion: at least I know there's no way I could have made that up. That was real. That was another dimension of reality that was so powerful.

I knew that the consciousness was love and light and that our planet had reached a point that it could hold that and ground it in the planet. Repeatedly, I would hear that we will make it; we are working toward giving birth to a higher consciousness and that this was one of the greatest symbols of it. But I couldn't really limit that to a definition of an archetype or non-human. I don't know what to do with it except that it was consciousness, which was love and light, which had come from—"come from"—I'm thinking spatially, but we had now connected with it. What I experienced I felt was our species' experience.

JM: You mentioned there were two other women there with you. Did they also share that experience?

BK: I worked with sacred plants that day and they were with me for that. We did the ritual for children together. They did not see what I saw. They heard—because I was singing what she said—but they felt something so powerful that they too felt that they had been transformed by that experience even though they weren't in that altered state of consciousness. It was a profound sacred experience that was almost frightening to them, but also very fulfilling.

They knew something profound had happened.

JM: I guess at that level the boundary between what's inside you and what's outside you sort of dissolves.

BK: Yes. The inside and outside. That was István's experience with Pisti too on several occasions; he would forget that Pisti had died. There didn't seem to be any boundary there. There was no division between the two.

JM: We're really touching on some very fundamental issues about the nature of reality throughout history. You and I have had many discussions about the historical vision of different mystics. The ultimate message I think has always been about oneness, that we are one with everything.

BK: Everything, yes. That's a powerful experience to have. When we come back and play our individual roles, we can kind of laugh and have a lightness about it, even our own faults and limitations.

I read about these beings, or these young children. I'm so grateful that so many children are coming in with a consciousness that I don't have. But it's not competitive. We don't feel less than because of whatever stage of development we are on. The whole experience is sacred and beautiful in its magnitude. Whatever level we are, that's where we do our work.

JM: It seems ironic because at some level the distinction between that which I'm imagining and that which is real seems so important to us at the human level, but if we're one with everything the distinction between reality and imagination becomes translucent.

BK: You've really said it. I mean that's a profound statement. That is so true, yes.

JM: I'd like to have the ability to give our readers a better handle on the interface between the collective unconscious and what the Tibetans called the bardo planes or the afterlife. At some level, Betty, I think that we may be moving into an area where we'll be able to define these things mathematically using the mathematics of hyperspace.

I don't know that we're going to get there any further through the realm of experience. You've had so many wonderful experiences, but they sort of leave these questions wide open.

BK: Yes, that's beyond my experience. I think that mathematics is a language that can describe the whole creation of the universe. Certainly, these archetypes, they're shapes. They can be seen mathematically too. I think all of it can and that is beyond my capability.

When we had these experiences, although I had studied Jung and the unconscious, the collective unconscious, I didn't think of it in those terms. I felt myself present in a reality that was so vast. Compared to what I'd lived my life in, my life seemed like a square inch. I said in *Miracle of Death*, I felt I had lived in one square inch of what is and called it reality. My experience was so much vaster than that. It was filled with love and awareness. Pisti's presence, of course, since he had died, that's what we needed: to be able to experience his presence, his consciousness continuing. Of course, his consciousness was larger than it was as a 20-year-old. He was always interested in those things, but on the other side his consciousness was what it could be there and was not here. I didn't think in terms of the collective unconscious. I did think in terms of archetypes, these powerful energy structures that help us to know what the universe is. I didn't think in terms of Jung's collective unconscious. When we think of the quantum sea, which we call the spirit world and the subtle world, the energy coming from pure intelligence takes the shape of an archetype. I had one experience in which I realized that this field has been misunderstood. I needed to understand that these archetypes within the field are living and that within one archetype there can be many individual beings who can then go back into that oneness of the archetype.

I have to say that I have questions when it comes to putting it in Jungian terminology.

I think also we talk about becoming conscious of these things and going on a journey and there are many structures. Certainly, in the cave cultures, they had some sense of transformation and journeys that would transform. And there were details that were given in the Egyptian and Hebrew traditions and with the pre-Socratics and so on. Then there was Joseph Campbell who talked about the hero's journey, or the alchemical structure for the journey. But when you get into the journey, everything starts happening and you can't exactly say there's stage one, two, three, and four. You're just plunged into it in a way and all kinds of things are happening simultaneously and before and after. I couldn't categorize it in terms of the collective unconscious.

And yet when we bring forth an archetype, it's because the species has reached a consciousness that brings forth that archetype. We know the nature of the quantum sea in our time and place through that archetype. I think that the archetype that was always after me was the feminine goddess, that female divinity. But that's what our whole species has neglected and has drawn forth from the quantum field in this archetypal form of the feminine being who is the earth, who is nature, the cosmos and soul at the same time. I think we are bringing forth that archetype collectively because we must have it.

One experience I had after Pisti died was when a shaman from South America came and wanted to work with San Pedro with István and me in Death Valley, and so we did. I had read myths in which a person who went to the underworld got stuck in the underworld. Well, I did. I experienced that. I was at a place of total symmetry, total balance and nothing could happen.

I experienced a strange happening: I felt an energy coming across the desert, this incredible sorrow and grief of the feminine archetype for what has happened on the earth to all the children. Certainly, I could pick it up because I was in grief for Pisti, but I knew this was far greater than anything I could possibly have experienced; the grief was so intense.

Later, I came to realize in my experience with Sira that she was the other side of that archetype. We had split it off. We had the ability to parent, to love, to have compassion and yet we didn't have the other side of its dimensionality, of its infinite aspect, of its continuation. That had been sliced off. What I experienced was that sorrow, the grief with nowhere to go. She screamed through my throat, "It can never be healed." Certainly, I had thought of all the people who suffered so much, they had to feel there's no way this can be healed—what has happened.

A few years later when I had an experience with Sira coming into me and embracing that half that had been split off, I realized that our species is trying to bring back the wisdom that was lost in Hebrew mysticism, that other side. We were told no one could see her [Wisdom, the divine feminine], that she had to go back to the other world because she couldn't exist here. I think the species is bringing her eternal dimension back and merging her with that sorrow, that horror, that disbelief, our ability to suffer but to see no meaning in it. I think what is happening to our species is that that is merging, that archetype is coming, it's finding its wholeness. It's been split off and now is a time when it's going to be whole. Our love and grief will no longer be split off from the eternal dimension.

JM: I'm very touched, Betty. You're speaking like a prophet, and I have no more words. I don't think there's anything we could say to add to what you have just said that's so profound and so important. I'm so honored to be able to share your prophetic words with our audience. I know we've done several interviews in the past. I think this one tops them all, Betty. What a joy, what an honor it is to be with you today.

BK: Oh Jeff, you know when I went through the desert experience, that almost killed me, feeling that screaming across the desert, that it could never be healed and knowing how many people have experienced that. It took me a long time to understand that experience. I had very many different views about it, then later the healing and the coming together. I think that we're all in that place where we long for that wholeness and that meaning and that purpose. I think, as a species, that is what we're working together to bring into time and space.

JM: Betty Kovács, thank you so much for sharing this wisdom with me today and with our readers.

8

Science and Postmortem Survival
with
Alan Ross Hugenot

⌒

Jeffrey Mishlove (JM): Hello and welcome. I'm Jeffrey Mishlove. Our topic today is science and post-mortem survival. My guest, Alan Ross Hugenot, is uniquely qualified to address this question. He has his doctorate in engineering. In addition, he is a near-death experiencer, a former board member of the International Association for Near-Death Studies, and he is a spiritualist medium and a minister trained at the Morris Pratt Institute from my hometown in Milwaukee, Wisconsin, as well as the Arthur Findlay College of Psychic Science in the United Kingdom. In addition, he is author of *The Death Experience: What It is Like When You Die*, and *The New Science of Consciousness Survival: And the Metaparadigm Shift to a Conscious Universe*. Welcome, Alan. It's a pleasure to be with you.

Alan Ross Hugenot (ARH): It's fun to be here. I enjoy answering questions for anybody that asks.

JM: You have a very unusual background with an advanced degree in engineering, a specialty in nautical engineering and a deep understanding of physics. At the same time, you're working as a spiritualist medium. I gather you're also credentialed as a spiritualist minister.

ARH: Yes. They used to have a TV show, *I Led Three Lives*. It's like I have two different personalities. When I'm operating as a medium it's similar to a different personality, but I'm not suffering from a multiple personality or something. Yet, it is very similar in a lot of ways.

JM: All of this really began for you in 1970—long before Raymond Moody first wrote his book, *Life After Life*, about near-death experiences—when you had what is very close to a classical near-death experience yourself.

ARH: Yes, that's true. It was difficult in the hospital at the time because nobody would believe me. At the time their standard procedure for anyone who had an NDE, was to label you as delusional; their cure being to send you to the nuthouse, the insane asylum, and keep you there until you shut up about it and pretended to buy into their view of the universe. They'd give you various drugs to get you to shut up about it.

The chief psychiatrist came to me and he said, "You think you died and came back and you're acting like you're Jesus or somebody. I mean, nobody can do that—." I responded, "now, you're a scientist. I respect all your degrees and all of your advanced learning. But, this is like I've been to Mexico, but your training does not believe Mexico exists. So, you insist on telling me I there is no such place as Mexico, so I couldn't have gone there? But, actually I've been there!

Instead of correcting me, you need to step up to the plate and say, "Hey wait a minute; let me find out about this. Where is this Mexico that I don't know about? And make a new discovery. But instead you're not doing your job."

Naturally, he didn't like this thinking so he wanted to commit me to the nuthouse. Fortunately, my orthopedic surgeon, who was a much more savvy individual, checked me out of the hospital all of a sudden one afternoon. In fact, he comes running in—I'm wearing a hospital gown—he puts me in a wheelchair, throws my clothes in my lap and takes me down the freight elevator to go out the back door.

I get put in my mom's car and we drive away still in the hospital gown, because the psychiatrists were trying to commit me that day to the local nuthouse. Honestly, it's very disconcerting to have the medical establishment tell you you're crazy when all you're trying to describe to them is what you actually saw and experienced.

I said, "I want to tell you about this," and they respond with, "You're nuts." It's as though you went to Niagara Falls and you're trying to tell somebody how wonderful it was and they don't believe you. It's not there, it didn't happen.

JM: Since you had that powerful experience, which I gather is one of the major milestones of your life, the field of Near-Death studies has really burgeoned. There's now an international association for near-death studies and many scientific papers have been published. You've served as a board member of that association.

ARH: Yes, that's true. I've written a lot of things about it. At IANDS we study it in great depth. The thing that proves to us that there is consciousness survival after physical death is the fact that all of these Near-Death experiencers are having the same experience—Raymond Moody says [they] are the twelve things that happen during an NDE—and we find in our research that each of the experiencers have parts of that classical description. They don't each have all twelve, but they will likely remember eight or nine of the twelve—.

Consequently, when they are all having the same experience, yet they've never heard of it before and they've never talked to anyone else about such a thing before it happens to them, then it must be the same recurring phenomena. Later, if they find IANDS they can get together and talk to other experiencers, realizing, "Oh, that's the same thing that happened to me." This rather precise correlation shows that an NDE is not a hallucination, and it's not something that's programmed into us genetically, but it is a real experience that they're having.

Dr. Pim van Lommel says it this way. "The brain doesn't work after about 30 seconds ... It just stops, when there is no oxygen, there's nothing going on, and it flatlines. Yet, if the patient has an experience that they remember when their brain is flatlined and their heart's not working, and there's no respiration, which means their physical body is basically "dead," by every definition of "dead" that we have, then that shows that survival of consciousness occurs with no support from a living brain.

JM: He's referring to cardiac arrest patients that he's studied. In your case, you were in a motorcycle accident but you hadn't suffered a cardiac arrest.

ARH: No, that is true. I was not pronounced "dead." Instead, I was in a coma and in the ICU. I was in that coma for twelve hours and that's when I had the experience. On the other hand, Dr. Van Lommel studies cardiac arrest patients after the fact because he can verify from the hospital monitoring that they were actually "dead." His study is what convinces scientists that what occurred to me, and what happened to the people with cardiac arrest, is a real out-of-body experience, where their consciousness is not supported by the physical.

JM: When we talk about the science of post-mortem survival, I've heard you make an interesting argument. It's really one of the most interesting that I've heard, and that is you refer to the law of conservation of matter and energy.

ARH: Energy is always there. $E=mc^2$; that combination of forces has to go someplace. Although the formula may have come apart, the components of the formula must still exist and so must go somewhere. Energy cannot simply disappear; it doesn't dissipate.

We now know that light energy (the part of the universe that we can currently discern) can go beyond an event horizon into a black hole and disappear from sight. But when it does that it doesn't cease to exist: it merely disappears. It doesn't stop existing; it's still there. Even if we can't detect it in the black hole it's still there.

Likewise, when your physical body dies and the life energy falls out of it. Where does that energy go to? What happens to that life energy, to that mind?

I love to go back to Max Planck who, clear back in 1900 said, "We cannot get behind this fact that the matrix of matter is mind." So, matter, our solid reality, is built on mind, that is the matrix on which the universe exists. Planck said that as early as 1900. He didn't know about near-death experiences, but he knew about the quantum and he was working on these things. Yet, his science told him that mind is what the whole universe is made up of and that we can't get beyond that.

We step back from materializing here or appearing in the physical, and instead move back into another part of our same universe—I'd like to call it dark energy, or the aether, but it is that 96% of the universe that we can not discern—but, we step back into that dimension and we drop the physical like taking off my jacket. That's what your physical body is, it's a jacket you just throw away; you don't need it anymore.

I like what Betty White says. Stewart White's wife Betty was a medium who later worked from the other side talking back to us here. *The Unobstructed Universe* is the book to read. Betty talks about two universes. There's the one we are stuck in over here in the physical, and then there's all the rest of it out here. She says, "I'm out in the rest of it (The unobstructed portion) and so I'm not obstructed by the physical like you are." In other words, she can go through a wall. While, we can't go through a wall, and bang up against it and we can't get past it. She goes right in through it and it doesn't bother her because it's not within her perceptive level at her vibration or her frequency. Her frequency is higher than that or lower than that, or something. Just like a radio wave goes through a wall.

JM: It sounds like with your background in engineering and physics and your work as a spiritualist medium that you think perhaps we'll arrive at a point where we'll have some sort of technology that will enable us to communicate with people on the other side.

ARH: That is my hope. Gary Schwartz has been doing some work at the University of Arizona on the cell phone: "soul phone" he calls it. He's able to get indications from what he calls "hypothetical people on the other side." He gets back definite signals from them. He's working on developing the signal transfer. He's got some pretty good stuff. Hopefully, we'll be able to use that someday. Yet, this has been the goal since Edison, who had this same goal also. Edison wanted to do this and so did Tesla. They were all trying to do create a telephone to the other side. No one has yet perfected an electrical or electronic gadget that's sold the rest of science on he idea. However, since we have discovered dark holes and dark energy, science is now realizing there's all this stuff that we don't know: 96% of the universe we don't know. So, all things PSI are suddenly back in the realm of possibility, and that is where the smart scientists are researching.

JM: Let's talk about your work as a spiritualist medium. You went to get formal training—this was sometime after your own near-death experience. You studied at various spiritualist schools to become accredited as a medium. You must have had some natural talent to begin with.

ARH: No, I think everyone has this talent. It's the sixth sense that most of us sort of ignore. When we come as children we actually have much more of it. But, as we assimilate into this society, we sort of put it in the back and forget about it and start using only our five senses instead. Children have imaginary friends and things like that. I don't know that they're so imaginary; I think they're just seeing on the other side. Anyway, I think we all have this talent and we can use it if we develop it.

When I began to approach retirement from the active engineering field in 2006, I decided that I would study mediumship because I knew we could go out-of-body as I did in my NDE. I knew that the people who were on the other side were just out-of-body like I had been. I also knew that lots of people had been telling scientists that they've been getting messages and information from the discussed relatives who were over there. So I decided, okay, I know they're there because I've been over there myself, so why can't we talk to them? And I decided to learn how.

I easily became a medium, because I already held the knowledge that the other side must be a reality. Consequently, It was quite easy for me to do this. Many people who are mediums believe they are "gifted." Yet, the truth is they're no more gifted than the next guy. They just are able to believe in its reality and have just sharpened their ability to intuit (their sixth sense). It is like a concert pianist sharpens his ability by practice. It is through practice that you learn. I found out that the Morris Pratt Institute offered a correspondence course, which took about four years back then. We had to read forty to fifty books and then report on them and know all about the whole background of spiritualism. I signed up for that course; I slogged through it, and I finished it.

Then, after I began to demonstrate the phenomena by receiving messages from the deceased, mediums that I worked alongside, people like Suzanne Giesemann, said that I need to go to Arthur Findlay College, which is in Essex England, in Stansted. I took their advice to heart and spent my own funds to go there several times, and it is like a graduate school for mediums. I have completed five weeks of intense study, including very advanced classes with Simone Key, the chief instructor. And, for a while during COVID, I continued with her over zoom. Instruction is nine hours a day and they feed you and house you on campus. It's very intensive. You go for seven days for nine hours a day, for a total of 63 hours of classwork in a week. At normal colleges you get three hours a week, for a total of 58 hours of class work in a semester. So, I have the equivalent of five semesters learning from some very learned mediums who have 30-40 years experience talking to the other side and they really know what they're doing.

In one class I was bringing through the grandfather of another girl in the class; there were about fourteen advanced students in this class. I said, "His name's Frederic and I see him wearing a three-piece suit and he's in Glasgow and he's working in a shipyard." Of course, at this point being a naval architect myself I'm thinking, "Oh, Alan, you're making that up." But I didn't say it; I just thought it in my head.

Yet, the instructor (Simone Key)—who's reading my thoughts psychically at the same time she is also reading the spirits' thoughts on the other side—she said, "Alan, he's not going to show up for the nurse over there in the back of the room. You're a naval architect. So, he's purposefully going to come to you if you're on the platform. You're not making it up. He's coming to you now *because* you are a naval architect and you worked in a shipyard, and will more easily understand him."

She said all that to me and I had never said anything about my doubts: she simply read my mind, just like we were both reading Frederick's mind. But, then Simone said, "Now tell me more about him."

So I responded, "OK, he works in the administrative department; he doesn't actually work out with the ships themselves." She says, "What kind of a house does he live in?" I started describing the house that he was giving to me—. But then Simone says, "What street?" I said, "Oak." I mean, Oak Street, good grief, this is the stuff that's coming through and she's teaching me how to reach out and get that information, which is just beyond my imagination. This is a real skill because it is hard to tell it from my imagination. Yet, through faith in my own intuition, I'm reaching out and finding that information that he's handing me; not questioning it, just taking it. I brought through a lot of information. Simone is the type of hard driving instructor who pushes you by saying, "So, is there a truck parked there. What's the license number on the truck?" That's the kind of intense training we go through to be an evidential medium.

I learned how to go beyond my ego and surrender to what's coming in. Now, speaking to you about it, I'm tearing up because I'm moving in that direction to that medium personality. Like I say, it's two different personalities and I get emotional and very intense. When I'm talking to you I'm trying to use what I will call "the professor." The other one is "the medium." The medium is a jellyfish, a pushover; it's so emphatic that I can't quite control everything. It takes over like that when I am demonstrating mediumship. But, that level of surrender is how you really get the good information, the evidence, which proves you are actually communicating with a surviving consciousness. It'll show you pictures; it'll show you all kinds of stuff. It's all in your imagination; it's happening in a certain little corner back here. It's happening in a certain place where your mind, your brain, changes visual things into words. That happens in what brain scientists call Broca's fissure, or something like that. That's where you do that reception. You change your thoughts, your visions, your symbols, into words that you then can say audibly.

JM: It sounds like what you're doing is at the conscious level. You're not going into a deep trance and losing consciousness.

ARH: No, I don't do that. I feel it all. It's a sensory thing. I feel a name. Now, how do you feel a name? People say, "That smell has a color." Yes, it does. It's at the same vibratory level. I FEEL NAMES. It's very hard to describe. People think the departed are going to tell you their name; say it in your ear. But, instead, I feel their name. I feel how they look. I feel the vision that I have of them and it's not auditory. It's totally feeling, totally sensory from right here [points to heart].

JM: You're describing how the information seems to come to your chest and how emotional it is for you when you do this mediumship work. I'm under the impression that many of the messages are all about love. People on the other side want to communicate how much love they feel for the people who are still over here.

ARH: That's absolutely true, Jeffrey. It comes into the chest area because of the chakras that are involved. It's a life energy. Consider that there are two kinds of energy. There's electro-mechanical energy and then there's life energy. Life energy moves from the heart chakra; it doesn't move from the brain. The brain hardly puts out anything at all but this area puts out all kinds of stuff and it takes it in and it's coming in here. Life has to do with love. Love and life are almost inseparable. They're bringing their love back for the people who are still living here and they're trying to share that. They use the life energy. It's a form of energy we haven't yet measured. It's in the dark energy somewhere. We will measure it one day. Actually, that energy may be a monopole in this physical 3D reality that we have, but it's most likely a bi-pole system with the other half of it on the other side.

We don't detect it here because we only get half of it. We detect something when we have both parts, the positive and negative. We only get the positive or we only get the negative, but not both. So, we've only got part of it. We don't get the whole thing so it's a monopole instead of a bi-pole.

When science learns how to detect the whole thing then we'll suddenly say, "Oh look at all this energy going around between people."

You can do it yourself already. For example, you walk into in a room, you feel a guy on the other side. He's in a bad mood, and you can feel it. That's the life energy that's moving. That undiscerned "life energy" is how they communicate with us.

When you love somebody you get a whole lot more of that. You totally can read them from across the room. You know exactly what's going on with them and it's all felt; it isn't said, it isn't visual, it's felt. That's how they communicate with us.

Likewise, when I'm being a medium I'm communicating to the other side. The person who is wanting to talk to them is here but they're not feeling it. All I do is feel it for them. It's like they're holding my hand while I'm talking to the other side.

I work through Helen. She's on that side. She's been there for over a quarter of a century and she talks to me because she knows me really well and she can make me feel exactly what I'm supposed to say to this person. I'm supposed to say, "I see a skier over there. He liked to ski, did he?" She's showing me something that reminds me of skiing so I'll say that. I was doing it for a girl named Angela one time and I had her fiancée who had died. Helen gave me basketballs. I said, "Oh, he likes basketball?" She said, "He doesn't even like sports." So, I couldn't figure that out. After the session was over I was talking to Helen—something I do every day at three o'clock in the morning—and I said, "Helen, what was that about with the basketballs?" She gave me this thought. She said, "His name was Jack. The one professional basketball player that you knew personally in your [life] was Jack Sigma of the Seattle Sonics. You knew him so I gave you basketballs so you'd think of Jack and then you'd say his name." To check this out I went back to Angela a week later and said, "Angela, was his name Jack?" She said, "No, it was Jacques."

So, Helen and I learn over time what symbols will make me do what. She can touch me and make me say things so I get the correct signal, the correct vision, and the correct symbol to say the thing that the sitter, the person that is trying to communicate to the other side will know, so I can bring through the name like that. If I could have said to Angela, "His name is Jack," she would respond, "No, it's Jaques, but that's him!" This is the type of detail that an evidential medium wants to come through; it put tears in the eyes of the receiver as they realize, "Wow, you really are connecting with my Jack or Jacques." That's how it's done. And it is a deeply emotional thing for the medium as well as the receiver.

JM: Helen is your spirit guide.

ARH: Yes, she's a spirit guide yet I've never met her in this life. She is my wife's mother and I met her daughter five years after she died and then I married her daughter. When I started doing mediumship, she showed up. Every time I go to a medium, here's Helen. I remember this one Danish girl was giving me a reading at Arthur Findlay College and she said, "Oh, that woman over your left shoulder there. Is her name Helen?" So I and my mother-in-law have a deep relationship. She always shows up and supports my every move.

One time I was working with another medium who knew about Helen. He said, "Oh Alan, I've got this woman but it's not Helen. Her name is Dorothy."

Well, that's her middle name. She sneaks up and she pulls this stuff off and there she is. People will say, "Oh, the medium is reading your mind," and all that. No, Helen shows up as Dorothy just so show that the medium is not reading my mind. She shows up every time I go to a medium. In the early times I would get information I didn't know about my Helen, my mother-in-law that I never met. So, I'd have to go to my wife and find out, oh yeah that's true, she did that. She'd be telling me something that wasn't in my mind, that the medium couldn't be reading for me, and then I'd go verify the fact later.

She works with me in communications with the other side. She's the medium over there; I'm the medium over here, and we're sitting next to each other. Then there's the departed soul sitting there next to her, and then there's the sitter who wants to talk to their departed loved one's soul. There's four of us in a row. Now, if we were at a party playing "whisper down the lane" the message might come out a little bit garbled on the other end, wouldn't it? In mediumship there is a lot of chance for garble to sneak in. Unfortunately, some people say, "Well, you're wrong," when your message is not 100% accurate.

One time I'm doing mediumship and I said to the woman, "I have your mother here," and I gave her the name. I'm talking about her mother by name. I said, "She loved cooking." The lady was a little distracted by her child playing or something and she said, "No, she didn't. She hated cooking. She was in service in a large mansion and she hated cooking. That's what she did for her whole life."

What the spirit had brought through was that she was a cook. I probably colored it by saying she loved cooking. I put that she loved it in there, because I love cooking. But, that's the garble that happens. Unfortunately, after I had given the lady her mother's name and that she was a cook, the lady decides I'm totally wrong because I said the words, "loved cooking." Her mom was a cook for her whole life. I had a fact here that was real, and yet the lady discounted the fact and said, "You're no good, you don't know what you're doing." She didn't believe in the connection anymore, and there it goes. If you go to a medium give them your full attention.

That's the hardest part of mediumship: to work with the people here and overcome their skepticism. I may get only half of the things right, yet I'm batting 500. Most professional baseball players don't bat above 250; they only get a quarter of it right but people think they are superstars. Mediums do twice as good as the baseball players, but people think they are incompetent. The truth is that sometimes I'm at 85 percent correct and there's only 15 percent that's garble in there. But, because of the garble people will jump up and say, "Not true, it's no good." For professional evidential mediums that's very disappointing. Why should we put ourselves on the line emotionally just so someone can condemn our few errors?

JM: I'm under the impression from people I know who have become spiritualists that probably the most convincing aspect for them isn't the information; it's the emotional connection. These people really believe that they are working through unresolved emotions, typically, that they have with their deceased parents.

ARH: I truly believe there is no retribution; there is only remorse. Suppose you were an SS officer in a Nazi death camp. What remorse you must have. How long does it take to work through all of that? When we first get over there, to the place the Catholics identified as purgatory, although it doesn't exist in that sense at all—. But, that temporary holding area does exist because we have to work through our personal remorse.

The near-death experience has the life review, which happens rapidly before they return to physical life. But, that NDE life review is just a foretaste of what goes on for a little while after we get permanently over there. Working through the remorse about this life so that we can move on from this life can take some time, and we may need to communicate our remorse to those we injured. We're still oriented and tied to this prior physical life while we work through that remorse. We look at everything we ever did. In a near-death experience, in the life review, you look at everything from the other person's side of the table, instead of your side. How did they feel when you said that? Why did you say that? You have to work all of that out for each individual after you arrive on that side.

I love what Francis Banks says. Frances Banks and Helen Greaves wrote a book in 1967 called *The Testimony of Light*. Frances Banks is the deceased soul who was writing back from the other side through Helen Greaves' mediumship. Banks says, you get two blueprints: how it should have been and how you did it. You look at those two blueprints and sometimes it's just devastating to look at it. She said that many people, when they first get to the other side, can hardly look at it. It's just so painful that they would rather do anything else, including just wait. Eventually they realize that they can't avoid this procedure. So, it may take some people a long time to work through the remorse because they have to look at everything.

Frances Banks also had an SS officer she talked about. She said the SS officer—this is transcribed in 1967 and it had been more than twenty years after world war two—had been just over in the shadows there with a Jewish lady that hated him because he killed her husband and children. But, her hatred kept her with him. She needed to release that hatred in order to move forward. Her husband and children were already over there, and yet she's been with this SS officer for 22 years, hating him; viscerally hating him. The SS officer is not ready to face his remorse and, because she can't move on, she missed out on spending time with her loved ones—time is different over there—but spending the time with her husband and her children is what she hated the SS officer for depriving her of. She has to go over why she's mad at him in order to move on. So, you can see that the remorse thing is very difficult. Some people spend fifty years over there. Other people get right through it because they say, okay, I've got to improve, and I have got to evolve. That's what it's like. If you want to know more about what it's like on the other side, do read that book, *The Testimony of Light* by Helen Greaves, 1967.

JM: I'm under the impression that time and space are very different over there and that also—maybe more important completely than time and space—is in this dimension of consciousness. I think you referred to it as a vibration.

ARH: It's a frequency. Our understanding of consciousness is now moving forward on the cutting edge of parapsychology; it's moving forward quite rapidly. We're making inroads. We're beginning to understand it. That part of the universe is entirely conscious. If you think about what Max Planck said, "mind is the matrix of matter." Matter can't exist except as "apprehended consciousness." We bring it into space and time and it manifests for us and we see it there. Think about the universe as appearing for you; from the dark energy it appears for you; it materializes in front of you the way you wish to see it. Some of that wish is corporate; we do it as a whole group at once thinking about how we want to see it. It materializes out of the dark energy. It annihilates and it comes back. This appearing and re-appearing is happening 23 septillion times a second. So, it's really vibrating. You think, well, I'm sitting on the chair, the chair didn't disappear. The truth is that "No, it did disappear, and reappeared, and came back again. It's re-materializing all the time for you, 23 septillion times a second. People say, how fast is that? It's hard to explain. But, as soon as you stop believing in it the chair will disappear entirely.

You have to realize, the universe appears around you and you can influence that. Consciousness is what the universe is made out of. Think about the string in string theory. Picture a string that's vibrating but there's no string there, just the vibration. That's consciousness; that's a "thought form." It has no physical reality. Yet, that is what the whole universe is built on: consciousness.

The universe is just a thought. Thoughts are things. Honestly, once you forget your skepticism and begin to understand all this stuff, all these esoteric metaphysical descriptions and language, suddenly, it makes more sense than physical reality. It all adds up and fits together.

JM: It sort of reminds me of the Cheshire cat in Lewis Carroll's *Alice in Wonderland*: only the smile is left.

ARH: The cat disappears and just smiles. That's a good way to describe it. I wish we could bring it to people: the Peace, which surpasses all human understanding. That's what comes, this super Peace. The Cheshire cat just sits there. The fool on the hill; he is so happy; he is so peaceful looking down at everybody. That's what it is. People say, oh, you're such a fool. Yes, that's right. I am the fool on the hill and it's a great place to be.

Then I shift back to the professor, from the medium to the professor, and I want to put this into a context people can understand. What I would recommend, and it may be ignored these days because it's a little difficult to work through but, if you want to understand, read: *The Betty Book* and *The Unobstructed Universe*, and the other books that go with it by Stewart White. They're in a series and they're just a great set of books, but what you need to read are those two. *The Unobstructed Universe* explains so much. You sometimes have to digress and go study some of the scientific terms. But, once you understand them, you find that Stewart and Betty are talking back and forth all the time and they put it in these scientific terms and you have to know what they are. But, if you will do the homework, it's a wonderful book: *The Unobstructed Universe*.

JM: It's a book that has been recommended to me for many decades, as a matter of fact. You wrote about your own near-death experience and you described it in very different terms. As I recall, you made the point of saying that here in the physical world we think of objects as being outside of ourselves. We study them, as you just described; we look up the dictionary definition. But on the inner planes you don't study objects or individuals; you BECOME THEM; you learn of them from the inside. When you encountered this being of light it wasn't so much you encountering the being as you becoming that being.

ARH: It was me returning to myself. I had known the "Being of Light" for eons. I've been around for eons, and here I am just bumping into myself. "Hi, there." "Oh, it's you." You see an old friend that you haven't seen in a hundred years, it's like, "Oh my, it's you. Hi."

It was like that. No introduction. Everybody says, "Who was it that you saw? Was it Krishna? Was it Jesus? Who was that? Was it Buddha?" No, it was just me and I'm back to myself. I'm home, home like you could never understand. We all want to go home, to the real place where we came from. That's it. I was there. I was home again.

Then I got this message from the Being of Light. You get it by ESP; you don't get it by hearing it. The message came, "You have to go back." I said, "No, I don't want to go back. I don't want to go back at all. I like it here. Let me stay right here. I'm home."

It all came as a feeling, but the being said, "You're not done. You're not done with what you were put there to do. You have a destiny. You must go back and fulfill it."

So I'm here and that's what I'm doing. The way that it works, it's always BECOMING. It's always about being but we have a feeling that we want to BECOME even more than JUST BE. Just be, I'm bored. I'm just being here. I'm bored. I want to BECOME. We want to grow; we want to go further. We want to discover more. That process of following the path *is* what life is. Life is the journey on the path. It is not about arriving.

I sail. I'm a sailor. When we're out in the boat and there's a little kid on the boat who says, "When are we gonna get there?"

the true sailors tell him, "We're there. We're sailing *now*." The little kid says, "No. When are we gonna get there? We're crossing this water. When are we gonna get there?"

Life is the becoming. We become all the time moving on that journey. The guides on the other side show me each step, one step at a time. I have to look at the step. The hard part is, there's the step and I have to take it. It's in front of me. I don't know what's coming but I'm gonna take that step. In each step, when you get to look back you can see what happened in hindsight: why it was that you took the step. You couldn't see it going in but you get to look back and see it.

Then, the next step comes, and again they've handed me another step. I have to take that step. If I try to figure it out I'll be wrong. I'll see this as an evil thing when it's a good thing or vice versa. I'll be wrong if I try to figure out. If I live in fear I'll wonder, "if I take that step what's going to happen?" We always try to second-guess ourselves. "I'm going to figure that out before I make that move." But, if you believe in source in providence, the move is there; the door is open; the window is open; take it, jump out the window. Go.

You will be absolutely amazed by what happens when you take the step. If you don't take it you're stuck; you're stuck in a box; you can't get over there; you're in a prison. But if you take the step, amazing things happen: things you could not have foreseen. Just going down that street, here comes somebody you needed to meet that you never ever would've met without that step.

I was watching a documentary on Westinghouse. When he went to Pittsburgh, the first day he is there he meets the guy that he spends the rest of his life working with: one of his investors. He's just walking up the street and he asks directions from the guy.

How did the guy get on the street? This super relationship comes out of this, "Hey, do you know how to get to the—?" There's the guy. When you look at life and understand the synergism that happens, that man was walking down the street so Westinghouse could meet him. It's just the way it was. There was Westinghouse; he got himself to Pittsburgh; he got on that street and he asked the question.

Those miracles happen; when you take the step the Universe shows you. If you don't take the step you won't be on that street and you won't see the guy. Instead, the fears of your conscious mind closed you off in this little box. So, you have to take the step.

JM: Of course, it's a different step for each person.

ARH: Yes, it is. We each have our own destiny, which is based a lot on who we are and how we're put together, our conscious state and where we're evolved to at the moment. Some people like to say we signed a contract. Instead, I like to say there were two blueprints. There was the one that could have been and the one that we actually did. It's all up to us with free will. It's not predestined with a contract that I *have* to do it. That's my destiny if I *choose* to do it, if I *will* to do it. The choice is always a free choice. We have free will. We're not robots being driven. We don't have to rob the bank. We wanted to rob the bank. When somebody says, "Oh, I couldn't help it. I robbed the bank because of the way my father treated me." No. We chose; we made the move; we robbed the bank. We can't blame someone else or something else. It's us that chooses; we have free will; we're not predestined.

The idea that the world is determinate, is something I disprove in my book: *The New Science of Consciousness Survival.* I take the first principles of physics and show how they're all presumptions and assumptions and how we can no longer uphold them with our quantum physics. Those 350-year-old presumptions don't fit. If we're going to believe in quantum physics and relativity then we cannot believe in the archaic science of materialism. They're not real. It was a hard one for Einstein. He worked on this all the time. He wanted to be a materialist and he knew he'd lost it and he couldn't go back there and he struggled with it. David Bohm and Einstein spent a lot of time trying to work it all out together at Princeton. For honest physicists, you need to read all of David Bohm's books. You need to understand the implicate order and the explicate order. You need to understand that there's the potential of the implicate order (the quantum field) and that this reality is the explicate order which we precipitate through the collapse of the wave function. We (you and I) precipitate the reality: we create the world that's around us, and we do it from the infinite potential. The whole universe is standing there as potential for each of us to develop that potential. Whatever we absolutely believe will just materialize and manifest in front of us.

I spend a lot of time trying to figure out how to say this to people, in ways that will make sense to them, that they are going to understand. People come up to me and they say, "I'd love to read your book, Alan, but could you put it into three or four sentences so I can just get it?" I say, "It's not like that. What you're saying is, "I'm too damn lazy to do my own homework. I don't want to learn. I don't want anything to change because I might have to learn a new software program in order to do the thing. I don't want to take the time to learn. I'm too busy." If you want the feeling and the peace that passes all human understanding and the confidence about life, that this is a wonderful life, you're going to have to do the homework.

Unfortunately, for those who want to hurry and short change it, the homework takes some time. I can't put it in three sentences. I might be able to put it in three volumes about three inches thick and put it all in there, but, because this learning is experiential and not intellectual, if then you will get on the path and take each step as it's put in front of you and do the homework, do the reading, do the looking up of the definitions to get it, and stop being lazy about it saying, "I'm gonna spend two minutes on this then I got to go somewhere." No, if you're going to go on this path you have to dedicate to the path. You have to make it part of you and then it'll begin to work; then you'll begin to get it and you'll understand it. Everybody wants to do everything so fast: an elevator to the top; do one thing just like that and it's all solved. But, they can't. It won't work. Personal evolution takes time.

JM: Let me ask you a tough question. Pretty much all the mystics, and I know you've been hinting at it yourself, will tell us that everything is one: it's all one; there's one consciousness and that's the universe. That being the case, why are we encapsulated in our own individual bodies? Why does it seem as if we're all separate individuals when we're really all one?

ARH: That's a great question. We've been asking that one for several thousand years. Why was this done? The best way I can try to explain that is, let's imagine that you're God. It's not a being like us. He/she experiences things, feels things. God is sitting there one day and has a thought: "I would like to know what it would be like to be the victim who was murdered. How does that feel? I would also like to know, how does it feel to be the guy doing the murdering? How does that feel? In order to do that I have to have a murderer and a murderee.

This brilliant consciousness, God, thought of all these billions of people doing all of these billions of things so he could feel all of that and see how all of that was. That makes sense to me. He/she wants to have it all and does this, creates the whole universe.

JM: Alan Hugenot, this has been a delightful conversation. We've covered a lot of ground here. What you've been saying reminds me of—I think it was Einstein actually, who said the most important question we can ask is, is the universe friendly? I've definitely got the impression from you that the answer is yes.

ARH: It's yes, if you see it that way. It's all about your perception. How do you see the universe? What does your culture give you that causes you to fear or love? If you see the universe as a wonderful loving place then that's what it is. If you see it as a terrible place, then that's what it is. It's up to you with your free will to choose that it's a wonderful place. And it is. It's a place of love; it's friendly; it likes us. Will it communicate with us? Yes, if we let it. What I would say to everybody in closing: if you fear death, start studying the things I'm talking about because I have no fear of death. My wife says, "Oh Alan, you can't wait." That's right. I was home and I want to go home again. That's how I felt when I was there. I was home. I did not want to come back here. When it finally comes—my ultimate you gotta go—I will be happy and grateful. I'm excited and I can't wait to get there.

Now, that's a much better way to look at death than to say, "Oh my god, I might die, I might die." No, I can't wait. I'm being patient. I've learned patience. I'm willing to live out my destiny, but I really just anticipate getting back there, where I was 52 years ago. It's a wonderful place. The universe is friendly. It does love us.

9

Alfred Russel Wallace and the Spirit World
with
Michael Cremo

Jeffrey Mishlove: Today we're going to explore the life and work of Alfred Russel Wallace. He was the co-founder of the theory of evolution together with Charles Darwin. Wallace was a spiritualist, and he was deeply involved in scientific investigations of 19th century spiritualism. Michael Cremo is the co-author of *Forbidden Archeology: The Hidden History of the Human Race*, and author of *Human Devolution: An Alternative to Darwin's Theory*: a Vedic alternative to Darwin's theory.

Michael, I'm so delighted that in *Human Devolution* you highlighted an interest in the work of Alfred Russel Wallace. He's a very important person in the history of science and particularly important in the history of psychical research and parapsychology. It's a crucial chapter in that history that's usually overlooked.

Michael Cremo: Yes, the actual history of Wallace is generally overlooked in biology textbooks as well. It's sometimes mentioned that he was the co-founder of the theory of evolution by natural selection along with Darwin.

Darwin had taken his voyage on the HMS Beagle. This ship journeyed around the world. Darwin was a naturalist and many of his observations such as those he made of the tortoises and the finches on the Galapagos Island originally suggested to him his theory of evolution. To summarize his theory, the idea is that species are not immutable types, but instead merge one into the other. After that voyage, he went to reside in the countryside in England. He began to formulate his theory and write a book about it. The book was later published as *The Origin of Species*. It took him a long time to write it: a couple of decades at least.

One day he received a letter from Alfred Russel Wallace. At the time, Wallace was a younger English biologist, or naturalist, who had been exploring in Southeast Asia. In his communication to Darwin, Wallace revealed he had come up with the exact same theory that Darwin was working on—a theory of evolution by natural selection. He enclosed in his letter a paper that he said was going to be read at a meeting of the Linnean Society, a biological scientific society in London. This was somewhat shocking for Darwin because even until today the etiquette in the scientific world is that the first person who presents a theory is awarded the credit of discovery and has their name attached to the theory via naming convention.

Darwin consulted with his scientific colleagues and asked them for advice on what he could do. They convinced him that the proper thing for him to do would be to ask Wallace if he would agree that a paper by him, Charles Darwin, would be read at the same time at the Linnean Society in London. That way they would both get credit for the theory. That was agreed upon. For a long time, the theory was called the Wallace-Darwin Theory, but you don't hear that very much anymore.

JM: A couple of years ago I was at the London Museum of Natural History and they had a special exhibit just on the work of Wallace. I take this as evidence that there's some effort amongst mainstream biologists to revive his memory.

I think he probably tarnished his reputation because he became an advocate of spiritualism. It's important to note as you did in your writing that he didn't start out as a spiritualist. He was, like Darwin, a materialistic 19th century Victorian who had no particular interest in spiritualism at all.

MC: Absolutely; when Wallace was in Southeast Asia he'd gotten sick and he was laid up in a hospital for some time recuperating. Reports began to come from Europe about Mesmerism, hypnotism, paranormal research and things like that. He was initially very skeptical about these things, but, when he returned to England, he began to look into the matter himself and he became convinced that there was something to it from the scientific point of view. He published a report directed towards his scientific colleagues on the topic of what he regarded as the scientific evidence for the supernatural.

JM: He attended many séances.

MC: Yes, he attended séances. For example, séances of a Mrs. Marshall; a Mrs. Nicholls; these were mediums, people with reputed paranormal powers that were providing demonstrations in private circles in England. He spent some time in these circles and the result was he concluded that there was something real going on here. He witnessed what he regarded as true examples of psychokinetic effects and levitations, among other things. He became personally involved in this research. This prompted Darwin to write him a very critical letter, which stated that by getting involved in these things "you're murdering our child," a theory which only made sense to Darwin in terms of a strictly materialist ontology.

JM: I think it's fair to say that the phenomena that most intrigued Wallace were some of the most bizarre inexplicable things: what we would call today macro-psychokinesis. This topic is still extremely controversial even amongst parapsychologists today because the sorts of things—materialization of spirit beings (an ectoplasmic form for example) or levitation of mediums themselves—these things today are extremely rare. Subsequently, modern researchers often think there must be something wrong with the accounts from the 19th century.

MC: Yes, that's a common reaction. However, I found it significant that Wallace didn't work alone. He worked in cooperation with other prominent scientists such as Sir William Crookes, who was later a president of the Royal Society, England's topmost scientific organization. Crookes was a physicist. He was involved in some of the work related to the discovery of the cathode ray tube and other endeavors centered in material science. He and Wallace were conducting experiments into the phenomena connected with mediums.

One of the mediums they investigated was Daniel Dunglas Home. Home had some interesting abilities. One thing Home could do was he could take an accordion and hold it with one hand opposite the keys and cause it to play elaborate tunes in that condition.

JM: Crookes placed the accordion in a cage to make it impossible for any sort of fraud to go on.

MC: Right! Even under those conditions he was still able to cause the accordion to play. Even more interestingly, he would withdraw his hand from the cage and, according to Wallace and Crookes, the accordion would float in the cage playing a tune. It sounds quite astonishing.

Another thing that was witnessed by both Wallace and Crookes were levitations performed by Home. We know that it's possible to manufacture the illusion of a levitation, but these events took place under circumstances that really completely ruled out those kinds of explanations.

JM: Stage magicians can do it when they're in control of the stage. To do it under scientific conditions with multiple observers who have strip-searched the magician and searched the room thoroughly is another matter altogether.

MC: You have to wonder, why did Wallace, the co-founder of the theory of evolution by natural selection, and Crookes, a president of the Royal Society, publicize these things to their scientific colleagues?

Did they have a psychological death wish?

Did they want all their colleagues to think they've gone completely off the deep end?

Or did they publish these things because that is what, as scientists, they observed?

Or did they simply think that other scientists deserve to have this information available to them? I choose the latter among those possibilities.

JM: It's also important to point out that it wasn't just the two of them either. There was a coterie, a clique of many prominent scientists from that era, who were actively involved in the Society for Psychical Research. Another one you mentioned in your book who was a colleague of Wallace was William James, the founder of American psychology.

MC: William James was a very interesting person because he was open to a whole variety of facts that would be looked upon quite negatively today. One case he investigated was what he regarded as a genuine case of spirit possession. The case is called the Watseka Wonder, in Watseka, a little town in Illinois. That was an interesting case involving a young girl named Lurancy Vennum. She lived a quite ordinary life until, at a certain point in time, she went into what she called trance states. In these trance states she claimed to be encountering the spirits of departed personalities.

One of the spirits she encountered was that of a girl named Mary Roff who had died previously in that same geographical locality. She reported this to her family members and they went out and searched for this Roff family. They brought her family to the Vennum house.

Lurancy had reported that in her encounter with the spirit of Mary Roff, this spirit being had told her, "I would like to visit my parents," or more or less, "I'd like to take possession of your body for a little while."

When that happened Lurancy Vennum began manifesting the personality of this girl, Mary Roff.

When the Roff family was brought to her house, Lurancy (now possessed by Mary) was able to identify them immediately without "ever having seen them before." By the agreement of both family members, she went to live with the Roff family and perfectly manifested the personality of their daughter as well as demonstrating all kinds of detailed knowledge about the family affairs that would have only been known to the deceased Mary Roff.

This went on for some months. Then she went back into the trance state and the spirit departed. Lurancy resumed her normal personality: suddenly feeling like a stranger in the Roff house, she returned to her biological family where she lived out the rest of her life in a fairly normal way.

I did find it extremely interesting that William James included this case in his textbook, *The Principles of Psychology*, as an example of what he regarded as a genuine case of spirit possession.

JM: I think it was removed from a later edition, but you're correct. The case was investigated by James' colleague, Richard Hodgson, who traveled to Watseka, Illinois, and interviewed the families some years later. It stands up as one of the most well attested and dramatic cases of possession, and not in the negative sense either because, as I recall, Lurancy Vennum was ill at the time and when Mary Roff manifested she stated that this would help heal Lurancy, which apparently it did.

However, the interesting point is that this case says a lot about your notion of human devolution. Specifically, the idea that humans from within what we could call the spirit world— or I call it hyperspace or some other dimension of reality, not conventionally what we think of as three-dimensional physical reality—are able to influence events in this world.

MC: Yes, and that depends upon understanding the actual structure of what a human being is ontologically. I think there are three things involved. There's a gross physical body made of the chemical elements; there is a subtle mental and intellectual body, and then beyond that there is the actual conscious self. I think what happens in these cases of possession is that you have a person, a conscious self who has separated from their gross physical body but has retained the subtle mental and intellectual body on some level of existence.

They are able to use their mental and intellectual form to take possession of the mental and intellectual body of a terrestrial human who is still embodied in a gross physical form. This may be done coercively or by consent. In this case the possession was by consent and the personality doing the possessing was benign. That said, there could be other cases with different circumstances.

JM: They're not always benign. Alfred Russel Wallace documented many, many dozens of different kinds of manifestations. For example, ectoplasmic materialization, where a spirit being seems to create a temporary body out of some mysterious substance called ectoplasm that is thought to exude from the body of the medium.

MC: He did observe things like that. I think that, ultimately, he considered that if there are mediums that can manifest those ectoplasmic forms then there might be higher beings in the cosmos that originally manifested, what we call species, the various forms that organisms take. I think it was part of his conclusion about evolution that things like that might also be involved, and I think this is why Darwin became very upset with him.

JM: I gathered that Wallace didn't really try to make that connection explicitly. He didn't try to modify the theory of evolution to incorporate the observations he had made working with spiritualists. But you seem to be pointing in that direction in your work.

MC: In part of my chapter about Wallace I look at how his parapsychological research influenced his thinking about evolution: especially, the evolution of the human form. He began to think there was something special about it that really couldn't be explained by the mechanisms that were involved in the production of other species. I think at least in that case he was somewhat willing to modify the mechanisms of the theory.

JM: I gather that, if I push you on your notion of human devolution, the idea might well be something like, at one time (maybe billions of years ago), highly evolved spiritual beings existing in a spiritual realm were capable of manifesting physical bodies that suited their needs and that may be how the first modern humans came into existence in our physical realm.

MC: Ultimately, I do think something like that. When I speak of devolution, I use the word in a few different ways. The primary way that I use it in this context is that what we really are in essence is conscious personalities, and the conscious personal self is not reducible to chemistry or physics. It has its own independent existence. I would say we all originally exist on a platform where we manifest a form of pure consciousness or spirit (in religious terminology). I prefer the term pure conscious self. In that sense, none of us are from the world of matter. We're from a higher realm. If we remained in that realm there wouldn't be any necessity for physical forms. It's only when we come to the world of matter that we require a vehicle that will allow us to function in this alien element.

It's like this, as humans we're normally meant to live on the land, but if we want to exist under the water for more than a few seconds we're going to need a vehicle that will allow us to function in that alien environment. You will need a diving suit or a submarine. Then we have to ask, where do those diving suits or submarines come from?

I would say they come from engineers who understand that if a human being is going to exist under the water, they need some type of vehicle that will allow them to do that. The engineers design and build those things to fulfill that desire.

But I would say, on the level of consciousness, there are beings that have the intelligence to manifest a kind of biological process. However, it is not one that we're familiar with.

It's more like what Wallace observed, mediums manifesting ectoplasmic forms that take on their own identities. Those forms are manifested by these higher beings in the cosmos. Conscious selves that want to exist on the level of matter are placed into those forms, which then go on to reproduce themselves.

JM: You point out in your book that Wallace himself didn't really explore the phenomenon of reincarnation, but subsequent researchers, such as Ian Stevenson, have accumulated massive documentation about cases where young children remember past lives. Very often there are biological concomitants to support the children's claims: birthmarks for example, that seem to reflect a time displaced historical artifact of the death wounds of a previous personality, can show up in the body of the present personality. This also suggests the ability of pure consciousness to influence a biological vehicle.

MC: There are some very interesting cases that Ian Stevenson and his colleagues investigated where they have shown that a personality may have died by a gunshot wound, for example, and it's known where the entry and exit wounds are. The living person who manifests the reincarnated personality of that deceased person will have a birthmark in the appropriate place of the entry wound and the exit wound of the deceased person.

This indicates that the mental body that accompanied that conscious self from one form to the next has retained that impression from their previous life. That subtle mental body will influence the physical body, configuring it in such a way that it will manifest birthmarks reminiscent of those wounds suffered in a previous life.

So, as you were saying, I would take that as evidence that a conscious self, through its mental body, can influence the form of the gross physical body. If that's true, conscious selves could also possibly manifest these gross physical forms on the first instance of their appearance on this level of reality.

JM: I should think that if Alfred Russel Wallace had lived long enough to be aware of that research, he would have found it very interesting. I'm so glad that we were able to both explore the history of Alfred Russel Wallace and also your own thoughts about the devolution of the human species.

About the Author

~

New Thinking Allowed host, Jeffrey Mishlove, PhD, is author of *The Roots of Consciousness*, *Psi Development Systems*, and *The PK Man*. He is the recipient of the only doctoral diploma in the world from an accredited university that says, "Parapsychology." It was awarded from the University of California, Berkeley, in 1980. He is also the Grand Prize winner of the Bigelow Institute essay competition regarding postmortem survival of human consciousness.

The New Thinking Allowed Foundation has recently launched a quarterly magazine. Copies can be downloaded for FREE from the New Thinking Allowed Foundation website, www.newthinkingallowed.org, and printed copies can be ordered from https://nta-magazine.magcloud.com.